C000178273

NORTH WALES
TRANSPORT

JIM ROBERTS

SUTTON PUBLISHING LIMITED

Sutton Publishing Limited
Phoenix Mill · Thrupp · Stroud
Gloucestershire · GL5 2BU

First published 1998

Copyright © Jim Roberts, 1998

Cover photographs. Front: Daily Mail sea plane lands
in Llandudno Bay, 1914. *Back*: Local bus outside
Ship Hotel, Aberdaron, Lleyn Peninsula, *c.* 1912.

British Library Cataloguing in Publication Data
A catalogue record for this book is available from the
British Library.

ISBN 0-7509-1722-9

Typeset in 10/12 Perpetua.
Typesetting and origination by
Sutton Publishing Limited.
Printed in Great Britain by
Ebenezer Baylis, Worcester.

Dedicated to my wife and family

The first aeroplane to land in Wales, Rhos-on-Sea golf course, 1910.

CONTENTS

There were no cameras around on 25 October 1859 when one of the most dramatic and dreadful events in Welsh maritime history occurred. A force 12 hurricane swept the western coast of Britain and 135 ships were sunk, 90 or more badly damaged and over 800 lives were lost. The loss of the *Royal Charter*, shown here in an engraving by an unknown artist, stands out among all of the other losses. This beautiful 2,719-ton steam clipper had been specially built at Sandycroft on the banks of the River Dee for the Australian Steam Navigation Company's fleet. She was the fastest and most famous ship on the Australian run and during the storm she went down off Anglesey. Only 40 people from a total of 500 passengers and crew survived this disaster. In addition to the appalling loss of life, the ship was carrying prospectors back to England and their riches were lost with them. Over £310,000 in gold was on board and many of the passengers carried their own personal 'stash' in addition. There was also a cargo of wool and sheepskins, and the estimated total loss was in excess of £600,000, by today's standards an enormous fortune. The boat had been forced on to the rocks at Point Lynas; she was broadside on to 60 foot waves and only yards away from safety. The inhabitants of Anglesey could only watch helplessly as the tragedy unfolded before them.

INTRODUCTION

Francis Bacon (1561–1626) said, 'There be three things that make a nation prosperous, a fertile soil, busy workshops and easy conveyance for men and commodities from one place to another'. Most historians would agree that an efficient transport system was an essential prerequisite for the development and success of the Industrial Revolution. G.M. Trevelyan (*English Social History*) says, 'Without improving communications neither the industrial nor the agricultural revolution could have taken place'.

In the nineteenth century the need for solutions to transport problems overland was particularly pressing. At a time when ships were carrying vast loads of goods around the world, coal and other minerals, for example, were carried in sacks strapped to the sides of pack animals, because wheeled vehicles would have stuck in the mud or come to grief in the ruts of the appalling road system then in existence.

In the intervening period between the departure of the Romans and the onset of industrialization, some fifteen hundred years later, no attempts were made to build hard roads in Britain. The work of the turnpike trusts was an attempt to remedy this deficiency but their work was piecemeal and left a great deal to be desired.

The lack of facilities made the movement of products of industry both difficult and prohibitively expensive; it restricted the size of the industries and the areas in which they could develop. Large-scale industrial expansion came about because of the development of the necessary infrastructure and new forms of transport; initially these were the canals and the railways, and only later the roads.

Communication systems in Wales have always been difficult because of its physiographical characteristics, and Wales has invariably lagged behind England when such developments occur. Whatever the development within Wales, the road, rail and canal systems have always been designed with communication with England in mind. The need for movement between London and Ireland was the paramount reason for the development of major road and rail arteries through Wales. It is as true today as it has ever been that it is easier to move in and out of Wales than it is to move within Wales. There is a particular divide between the north and south of the country, and recent road structures underline this point. The M4 corridor in the south of Wales and the A55 in the north are both roads designed for rapid transit into and out of England. Similar conditions apply on the railways, and passengers travelling from North Wales to South Wales or vice versa more often than not have to travel via England to complete the journey. The development of the A470 to link north and south is a proposition replete with problems since it passes through some of the most beautiful and environmentally sensitive countryside in Great Britain.

This book attempts to portray the early years in the development of transport within North Wales, looking through the lenses of the many photographers who have recorded aspects of this growth on land, sea and air. For convenience the book has been divided into chapters but it must be remembered that the true transport revolution was the result of the interaction of the systems as they occurred simultaneously.

These views, dated *c.* 1910–12, show Telford's 1827 road around the magnificent promontories of Penmaenbach and Penmaenmawr. This road replaced one built by an engineer called Sylvester in 1772, which was lower down and extremely dangerous, threatened by the constant battering of the sea and the fall of.rocks from the overhanging cliffs.

CHAPTER ONE

ROAD & RAIL
INFRASTRUCTURE

Before road and rail communication into and within North Wales could become a reality many natural hazards had to be dealt with, and major problems were faced by the early civil engineers. The rivers Dee and Conway have proved troublesome throughout history, and the strait between Anglesey and the mainland was for centuries a major headache. Rocky promontories on the coast and mountains inland have presented considerable difficulties. The photograph encapsulates the problems at Conway with Telford's Suspension Bridge jostling for space with Stephenson's Tubular Rail Bridge and the relatively recent 'new' road bridge.

From 1743 until 1897, the provision of a free ferry was obligatory at Queensferry on the River Dee. The ferries were chain ferries pulled backwards and forwards by chains passing over a windlass. In 1897, the date of this photograph, the first Queensferry Bridge was opened. It was the year in which Queen Victoria's Diamond Jubilee was celebrated, and the bridge was named the Victoria Jubilee Bridge. It extended over 400 ft and the central span divided and moved under a fixed road. The original road was made of wooden blocks, later replaced by Buckley bricks. The designer of the structure was W.T. Barber, and people crossing had to pay a toll.

In 1921 the Jubilee Bridge was found to be unsafe and was scheduled for demolition. Work began on a replacement in 1925 and the building was completed in October 1926 at a cost of £78,377. Here it is near completion. Despite this bridge the roads in this area have been constantly congested. A new motorway bridge has been constructed and has provided some relief but traffic problems through Shotton and Connah's Quay persist, and in 1997 work is in progress on a bridge over the Dee which bypasses these trouble spots.

For centuries the crossing of the River Conway was a hazardous ferry journey because of the tidal conditions. A long diversion up river to the bridge at Llanrwst was an alternative route until a bridge was built at Tal-y-Cafn. Increasing traffic from England to Ireland through Holyhead meant that a good land crossing was desperately needed. Telford's road from Chester to Holyhead made a bridge crossing even more pressing, particularly as proposals were afoot for crossing the Menai Strait. In April 1822 work began on Telford's Suspension Bridge and four years later on 1 July 1826 the bridge opened. Stephenson's Tubular Rail Bridge was a forerunner, and experimental trial, for the much bigger tubular bridge across the Menai Strait. The new road built in the 1950s accelerated the crossing of the river but produced major congestion in the town of Conway. This self-inflicted problem was solved in 1991 when a tube was immersed in the river to take the large amount of coastal traffic away from the town.

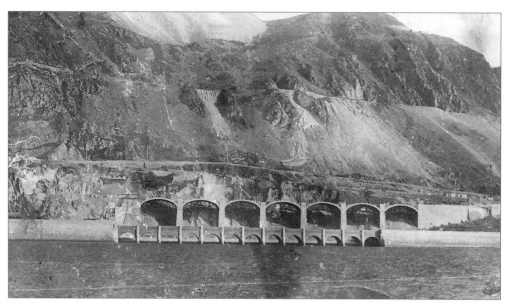

Large-scale construction work from 1931 to 1935 realigned the road around Penmaenbach and Penmaenmawr. Seven arches were built to carry the new road above the rail track and below Telford's road. Two tunnels were blasted through the granite. The whole venture was necessary to accommodate increasing pressure on the route. The seven arches are clearly seen in the view above which was taken from the sea. Granite from the quarries which so injure the environmental beauty of the area has been used in buildings and roads all over Great Britain. The photograph below shows the road and rail configuration, and its proximity to the sea. It is clear that a great deal of buttressing had to be used to support the road structure.

One of Telford's greatest engineering achievements, the Menai Suspension Bridge, was built in the early years of the nineteenth century. Before the bridge was built there were six ferry links between the mainland and Anglesey. It was built at the narrowest point of the Strait and also the most sheltered. The line of the main Chester–Holyhead road was also close. The bridge cost £123,000 to build and construction took seven years. The first mail coach drove over the bridge at 1.30 a.m. on 30 January 1826 and on that day many thousands of people crossed on foot. The suspended span was 579 ft, 100 ft above the surface of the Strait. The original was built with the needs of horse-drawn vehicles in mind, and when increasing pressure from motor vehicles, in terms of speed and weight, became evident it was necessary to strengthen the whole structure. Between 1938 and 1941 the ironwork was replaced by steel and the four main suspension chains were replaced with two stronger ones, as seen in the photograph above. Below, in a photograph of about 1870, the four chains are visible with the central walkway for pedestrians. Horse droppings have been replaced by petrol and diesel fumes as the major pollutants since then.

The last rivet was hammered home on Robert Stephenson's amazing engineering feat on 5 March 1850 after four years of arduous and dangerous work. Two wrought-iron box girders weighing 10,500 tons and stretching 1,470 ft made up the Britannia Tubular Bridge. Optimum space was provided beneath the girders for busy shipping traffic through the Strait. The clear rectangular openings were 450 ft wide, with a minimum high water clearance of 105 ft. The lions at the entrance were 25 ft long, 12 ft high and weighed 30 tons. They were made of limestone quarried in Penmon quarries, Beaumaris. A proposed gigantic figure of Britannia on the central tower was abandoned when the cost was realized.

ROBERT STEPHENSON, ENGINEER.

An early suggestion for the rail link with Anglesey was for trains to be pulled by horses on specially constructed wagons across the Telford Suspension Bridge, which would then link up with a rail system on the other side. This was clearly a time-consuming and impractical proposal for a system which was supposed to speed up the mail service to Ireland. The two photographs on this page show the 'Irish Mail' on its journey towards Holyhead and the packet boat service across the Irish Sea.

This was the last photograph taken inside the Tubular Bridge, the day before the disastrous fire of 22 May 1970 which led to its demolition. Children had used a lighted taper to explore the interior for bats, so it is said, and the tarred roof burned with an intense heat which warped and twisted the metal box girders. The inspection team is W. Nobis (engineer, HQ Euston), T. Schofield (asst. engineer, HQ Euston), F. Roberts (stonemason, Bangor workshops) and K. Aitkin (chargehand stonemason, Bangor workshops).

After the fire. An inspection team is assessing the extent of the damage. Among them from left to right are: Harry Williams, Now Jones, Jack Pritchard, Emrys Roberts, Bob Goodman Jones, Neville Robinson, Richard Rowlands and Will Lloyd Jones. A detailed inspection revealed extensive structural damage with the tubes precariously perched on the towers and requiring urgent, temporary support. The Royal Engineers provided immediate assistance and helped considerably in the aftermath of the disaster.

After the fire, it was clear that the box spans had a considerable sag in the middle. The Anglesey side span sagged almost 3 ft, and the connecting points with the towers had also been badly damaged. Arches were built under the box girders and the wrought-iron tubes were cut into sections and drawn off the bridge by train. The main feature of the new bridge (below) is the replacement of the original spans with steel arches. These were prefabricated at Port Dinorwic and floated 4 miles down the Strait to the bridge for erection. The bridge was now sufficiently strong to carry a roadway over the railway, thus providing a much-needed second road across the Strait. It carries only a single-track rail, but sophisticated electronic automatic controls allow for twelve trains per hour to cross the bridge.

In 1810 the Post Office asked Parliament to consider improving the whole of the road system from London to Holyhead in order to expedite transport of mail through North Wales to Ireland. In 1811 a survey of the route was undertaken by the 'Collosus of Roads', Thomas Telford. The work of twenty-three turnpike trusts had to be inspected and boosted. In North Wales the route ran from Shrewsbury through Corwen to Capel Curig and beyond, a stretch of road described by a Parliamentary Committee of 1817 as 'in the worst possible condition'. At the same time the repair and improvement of the northern coastal route through Chester was undertaken. By 1830 the Holyhead road was virtually complete, which led to a massive increase in the number of wheeled vehicles through North Wales. The 'coaching age' had begun. Then the railways came along and, by mid-nineteenth century, the coaches had given up the struggle. Above is the graceful Waterloo Bridge at Betws-y-Coed on the Shrewsbury–Holyhead road, built in the same year as the Battle of Waterloo. Below is the route through the Nant Ffrancon Valley between Capel Curig and Bangor, showing the mountain terrain through which the route has to pass, and the sheep hazards which are also a feature.

CHAPTER TWO

HORSE-DRAWN
VEHICLES

Wheelers' Coach at Betws-y-Coed, which conducted a circular tour of this beautiful and popular part of North Wales.

At the turn of the century horses reigned supreme on the roads of the world. A huge infrastructure existed to support this method of transporting people and goods from one place to another. Stabling, watering, shoeing, feeding and caring for horses was a massive undertaking, especially in large cities where thousands of people were employed on these tasks. Photographs of central London in the early decades of the century show the traffic congestion caused. Imagine what it would be like if every passing motor car was a horse-drawn vehicle. The problems of pollution would be different, and prize vegetables and roses would be commonplace.

A sight-seeing tour by horse-drawn coach was a required item of any holiday itinerary. 'Four in hand'
tours, as seen here in St George's Crescent, Llandudno, were advertised all over the town, with
excursions to Bodnant Gardens, Swallow Falls and Snowdonia. The fare from Llandudno to Swallow Falls
in 'The Rocket', with rubber-rimmed wheels, was 7s. The 'Prince of Wales', a larger vehicle, left
Llandudno at 8.45 a.m. and arrived at Betws-y-Coed at 11.15 a.m. for a light lunch and then on to the
mountains of Snowdonia. Road conditions and primitive coach springing ensured that the passengers ate
standing up for several days afterwards.

At the foot of the Sychnant Pass at Dwygyfylchi passengers are boarding the coaches in a busy holiday
scene.

The popularity of the scenic tour can be seen clearly here in a postcard published in 1908. Six vehicles of varying sizes are on the Sychnant Pass above Penmaenmawr. In all there are approximately 100 people on these coaches enjoying the splendour of the North Wales scenery and providing seasonal employment for the drivers and attendants.

A horse fair at Llangefni on Anglesey was held regularly and provided a valuable service for the rural community, which relied so heavily on the horse for transport and heavy labour. The fair was held in Church Terrace, Llangefni, as this provided a stretch of road in which the horses could be run for effective appraisal by prospective buyers. This photograph was taken in 1906.

When the occasion calls for ceremony it is difficult to improve upon the horse for adding dignity and atmosphere. These photographs were taken in the streets of Caernarfon in about 1908. The High Sheriff of Caernarfonshire, C.G.D. Assheton Smith Esq. DL, is in procession to the assizes at Caernarfonshire Crown Court. Mr Assheton Smith's family had quarry interests in the area at the time. They were a very influential family in the history of Caernarfonshire and were responsible for the building of the Snowdon Mountain Railway.

One of the advantages the internal combustion engine had over the railway was that goods and people could be transported from door to door without the need for an intermediate carrier. The railway horse and cart was a common sight on the streets into the 1930s. These two photographs show magnificent 'station horses' at Bangor above, and Caernarfon below; in the lower picture it would appear that redundancy notices have been served, in 1931. Before the advent of petrol-driven wagons many large stations used coal-fired steam wagons to transport goods, as will be seen later.

Greenfield's coal merchants at Colwyn Bay with a beautifully turned-out rig, *c.* 1914. The horse is bedecked with brightly polished brasses, bells and ribbons. Behind the children on the wagon there is a very large lump of coal. The poster behind Mr Greenfield is advertising Rhyl's May Festivities, so it is reasonable to assume that the ensemble is en route for a May Day Parade in Colwyn Bay.

Preparing for another May Day Parade are the staff of Edward Owen, joiner, builder and contractor of Back Madoc Street, Llandudno. Behind the wagon are the premises of someone who relied on the horse for his living, P. Williams, saddle and horse-collar maker.

Betsy Jones was a very well-known baker and confectioner in Llangefni, Anglesey, at the turn of the century. This photograph was taken in 1910 when this type of two-wheeled van was common. The back of the van was fitted with trays which contained the homemade bread and cakes.

Around 1900 the connection of houses to mains water supply was, to say the least, erratic, and the purity of the supplied water was sometimes questionable. The photograph above, taken in Holywell in the early years of the century, shows the locally famous blind water seller Joe Barker, who roamed the streets of the town with his helpers, selling pure well water for human consumption. Despite his blindness he is reputed to have had a prodigious ability to count money; he charged 1*d* a bucketful, or the barrel was yours for 2*s*.

A scene on Llandudno beach with two early perambulators, *c.* 1910. The reason for including this photograph in this section may become clear when the next photograph is examined. The caption for the whole page might read 'From the cradle to the grave'.

Llangelynin Church is situated in a quiet, remote and lovely setting in the hills above the town of Conway. Its remoteness meant that it was not easily reached by road in the early years of this century; consequently the ancient two-horse bier carried the departed to their last resting place.

CHAPTER THREE

TRAMS

The towns of Llandudno and Colwyn Bay were connected by a tramway between 1907 and 1956. The very
popular electric 3 ft 6 in gauge line operated a frequent service, which started at the West Shore terminus,
Llandudno, ran through Gloddaeth Street, the centre of the town and Bodafon Fields. It traversed the summit
of Penrhyn Hill through Penrhyn Bay and Rhos-on-Sea into the terminus at Colwyn Bay. Between 1915
and 1930 there was a single-track line from Colwyn Bay into Old Colwyn. The company had the longest
route mileage and the biggest car fleet in North Wales.
The inadequately financed company could not cope with the need for modernization and, since it was
before the time of 'tramway preservation', the local authority was content to see the tramway deteriorate
in favour of the roads and buses.
This photograph taken on 19 October 1907 shows the first official tram, No. 14, on the route. A limited
experimental service had been in use since 26 September 1907 after a Board of Trade inspection.

Gloddaeth Street, a wide airy road bisecting the Creuddyn Isthmus, is an important road in Llandudno as it connects the North and West Shore. The tram in this excellent photograph of 1910 is on its way to the West Shore terminus, where there is a beautiful circular tram station, created in 1907 and recently restored by Llandudno Council. In the background the paddle steamer *La Marguerite* has just left the pierhead and is on her return journey to Liverpool.

This mixture of street traffic is indicative of an era of transport transition. Horse-drawn vehicles share the roads with an electric tram and a petrol-driven car parked outside one of the hotels. The tram is approaching the sharp bend into Mostyn Street, the main shopping thoroughfare.

Passengers board car No. 5 on its way to the West Shore terminus. Car No. 15 (ex-Bournemouth) is approaching the sharp bend into Mostyn Street. The screeching of the trams at this point was, at one time, a cause of great concern, but it was said to have been cured by the liberal application of grease to the rails.

Car No. 6 of the original fourteen single-decked stock purchased in 1907 is approaching Hooson's Corner outside the Carlton Hotel in Mostyn Street. The tram will soon swing left up Gloddaeth Street and Gloddaeth Avenue to the West Shore terminus. The town crier's cart is to the left of the tram and another tram is nosing around the corner into Mostyn Street. Tram No. 6 left the service in 1945 after being renumbered 16 in 1936.

The busy intersection between Mostyn Street and Mostyn Broadway. The Broadway Hotel is on the left, and the North Western Hotel (now the Castle Hotel) is on the right. Car No. 13 is entering town and the toast rack No. 20 is on its way down Broadway towards Craig-y-Don. No. 20 was built in 1920 and stayed with the company until 1956. The open-topped double decker No. 13 was purchased from Bournemouth in 1936 and also served until 1956.

The tram on the left, seen just above the wall, is leaving Bodafon Fields and crossing Nant-y-Gamar Road into Craig-y-Don.

A public right of way crosses the line at this point, with an access stile to the left of the tramway shelter. The route takes on a distinctly rural aspect here through Bodafon Fields. Tram No. 15, acquired from Bournemouth in 1936, is approaching Craig-y-Don.

Toast rack No. 19 climbs the relatively shallow gradient on the Llandudno Bay side of the Little Orme, with the Great Orme in the distant background. The driver, who is accompanied by a driver colleague, is Mr Robert Cain.

The beginning of the end! There was considerable rivalry between the Crosville bus company and the tram company. The vehicles frequently raced one another to reach designated stops first for passenger pick-ups. In this photograph of the early 1950s we see a Crosville-owned Bristol Lodekka and tram No. 2 on Bryn-y-Bia road on Penrhyn Hill. The tram company, after closure, tried to revive its fortunes by setting up a 'Red Bus' service. The last red bus ran into the Rhos depot on Saturday 27 May 1961 and on the following day Crosville bought the 'goodwill' of the tram company for £40,000.

Tram track, Little Orme, c. 1910. A shelf cut into the side of the Little Orme provides a ledge on which the tram track was laid. The gradient at its steepest here was 1 in 11, and descending required great caution, involving the combined efforts of driver and conductor. There has since been considerable housing development and a complete main road realignment in this area.

Car No. 4 at the foot of Penrhyn Hill, *c.* 1910. Driver, conductor and inspector are posing for the photograph which was taken and published by G.R. Thompson, the self-styled Postcard King of Llandudno. Centre left is Penrhyn Old Hall, one of the oldest buildings in North Wales with its own private chapel, now disgracefully neglected! Above, in the background, is Penrhynside village, once the home of the quarrymen who worked in the Little Orme limestone quarries.

Car No. 3 at the foot of Penrhyn Hill on the main road route into Llandudno. This is now a dual carriageway. In this photograph the route for normal traffic is on the left.

The normal traffic route into and out of Llandudno has been quite considerably built up since the previous photograph was taken. At this point now four lanes of traffic provide access to Llandudno Bay.

Skirting the shoreline at Penrhyn Bay, the tram route has left the steep slopes of the Little Orme behind. This stretch of the track presented many difficulties over the years, the rail foundations being constantly eroded by the sea at high tide. The area is very little developed in this photograph. A road with a large sea wall defence now covers the area shown.

The Penrhyn Bay stretch of track was notoriously difficult to maintain, being subject to damage from heavy seas and high tides. Attempts were made to obviate these effects by dragging boulders up the beach to act as breakwaters, but the task presented great logistic and financial difficulties, and was stopped. Eventually the seaward track was left untended, as in this photograph, and single-line working ensued. The outer track was eventually obliterated when the sea wall was constructed in 1953 and single-track working continued for the remaining three years of the company's existence.

Tram No. 6 is on the passing loop adjoining the Rhos-on-Sea golf course at Penrhyn Bay. A toll gate was built here in 1909 by William Horton who set it up to pay the taxes imposed by Lloyd George's Pensions Act of 1908. It was known as the 'Budget Toll Gate'. The tram company bought the route in 1911 and collected tolls for fifty-two years until they were abolished in 1963.

A crowded toast rack outside the Caley Arms in Rhos-on-Sea is returning to Llandudno. This tram is part of the original toast rack stock built for the company by the English Electric Company Ltd of Preston in 1920. The trams lasted until the company's closure in 1956. The driver here was popularly known as 'Farmer Dick'. The conductor was Frank Jones.

An ex-Bournemouth, No. 13, purchased in 1936, is on the front at Rhos-on-Sea. This vehicle was built in 1921 and completed forty-five years' service with its two owners before being withdrawn in 1956. Rhos pier in the background was demolished in 1956.

Car No. 8 is moving down Conway Road in Colwyn Bay town centre on its way back to Llandudno. This car was built in 1907 and was withdrawn from service in 1936. This quiet main street is now, of course, choked with traffic most of the time.

The route was extended to Old Colwyn in 1913 but before this happened this was the busy terminus at the top of Station Road in Colwyn Bay. The steamship booking office on the left has attracted an Edwardian crowd. The absence of motor traffic makes jay-walking less hazardous than it would be today.

In 1913 the company decided to extend the track into Old Colwyn. In this view of about 1918 one of the original cars is on the track in Abergele Road, Old Colwyn, returning to Colwyn Bay and Llandudno. The extension was in operation into the early 1930s when it was discontinued and taken over by a limited local bus service. Plough Cottages with their distinctive semicircular garden walls have now been demolished.

The open-topped double decker No. 8, purchased in 1936 (ex-Bournemouth 116), was chosen to be the last tram on the route; it is being driven by Inspector Fred Wooley and a party of drivers from Bournemouth, who took it in turns to drive over the whole route. In the thirty years of the company's existence they were reckoned to have carried over 130,000,000 passengers. There were several reasons for the demise of the system: problems associated with financing the electricity supply from MANWEB, competition from bus companies, and increasing use of the private car. The roads were also becoming congested. This photograph was taken on 24 March 1956, a day on which hundreds of people took their last tram ride, and a crowd sang 'Auld Lang Syne' outside the Rhos depot.

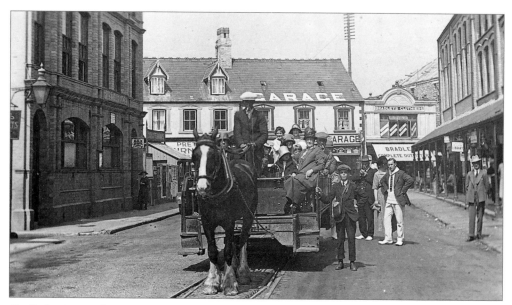

On Friday 28 October 1927 a driving sea and a freak storm washed away the small tram system which had existed on the front at Pwllheli for thirty-one years. Initially it had been a track used for transporting building materials for the construction of a hotel, houses and holiday facilities at Pwllheli's West End. Solomon Andrews & Son of Cardiff decided that the track could be modified to transport tourists and holiday-makers. The track consisted of flat-bottomed rails spiked to sleepers with a gauge of 3 ft. In 1896 Andrews purchased Glyn-y-Weddw Hall and decided to convert it into a holiday attraction. The tramway was extended to Llanbedrog and central Pwllheli sometime in 1897. Above, the occupants of a high-sided open car pose for the camera outside the post office in the West End. Below, an early view of the West End terminus with both open and closed cars. The photograph was taken before the opening of the depot. When Pwllheli Corporation saw the success of Andrews' system it decided to copy it and in 1899 it opened a small horse-drawn tramway from the town centre to the South Beach. This had little commercial success and closed in 1918–19.

Between 1876 and 1927 a tramway system existed at Wrexham. Initially the system was a solitary horse-drawn car on a 3 ft gauge track, but two more cars were added later. The route was Wrexham–Rhostyllen–Smithy–Johnstown. In 1901 the last horse-drawn journey was made, and horse-drawn buses took their place while alterations were being carried out. The track was widened to 3 ft 6 in, extended to Rhos High Street and overhead electric wires were put in place. In 1903 the electric line opened, the first in North Wales. In the 1920s the buses began to take custom away, which led to the closure of the system. The company, which had boasted ten cars in its heyday, closed on 31 March 1927. Above, an electric car stands outside Albion Brewery in central Wrexham with Wrexham's famous parish church, one of the 'Seven Wonders of Wales', in the background. Below, a photograph of 1903 shows the new depot. The destination boards from left to right read: Rhostyllen, Johnstown, Wrexham Terminus and Rhos.

The Great Orme Tramway opened on 31 July 1902. There was not too much pomp and ceremony on the occasion: a small crowd gathered to cheer as the town band played 'God Save the King', and thus the longest funicular (cable) railway in Great Britain opened for business. Within about two months it had carried 70,000 passengers halfway to the Orme's summit. The assembly above consists of the directors of the company and the tramway staff on the day of the opening. They are standing at the halfway point on the line. The top section was not opened until 8 July 1903. The photograph below was taken much earlier and shows the route the tramway took towards the summit. In the background there is little town development.

The route starts here at the Victoria station, which derives its name from Victoria House, demolished in 1901 when work began on the tramway. Soon after leaving the station the line runs very steeply through a narrow passage leading to the Black Gate. The gradient is about 1 in 4.4 and at one point is 1 in 3.6.

A danger point on the line, controlled by traffic signals, is where the line crosses Old Road and Tygwyn Road at the Black Gate. This photograph clearly demonstrates the steepness of the gradient on this part of the route.

At the top of Tygwyn Road after the Black Gate there is a passing loop seen here with trams Nos 4 and 5. The poles on the top of the cars are for telegraphic communication and are not power units. Nowadays the operators communicate by radio. The first half of the system is 872 track yd between Victoria station and the halfway station, which is 400 ft above it. The system is in two sections because the distance is too long for one cable to operate.

Another passing loop, but this time on the less steep part of the route to the summit. Passengers had to change trams at the halfway station, which can be seen in the distance. The smoke shows that the photograph was taken when steam power was used to drive the two colliery-type winding engines. In 1957 there was a change to electric power, which was cheaper and far less troublesome. Just before this the engines burned 250 tons of coke a year at a cost of £7 a ton. The lower section engine with the steepest haul is 120 hp, while the upper section engine is 60 hp.

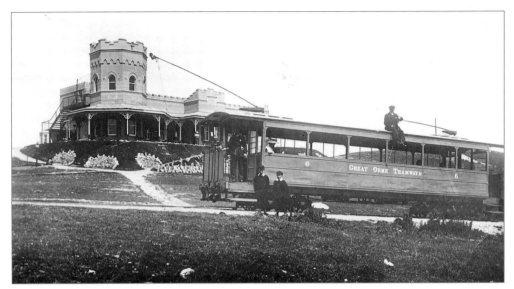

The upper, less steep, half of the track is 827 yd long and terminates just below the summit, 679 ft above sea level. Cars 6 and 7 operate on the top section and 4 and 5 on the bottom section of the 3 ft 6 in gauge tramway. In the background of this photograph is the Summit Hotel, which has had a chequered history. Passengers are now free to take in the magnificent views over the Conway Estuary and the hills of Snowdonia, and, to seaward, perhaps a glimpse of Ireland and the Isle of Man.

On 23 August 1932 an accident occurred which almost led to the closure of the tramway. When car No. 4 was descending the steepest part of the track a draw bar snapped, the brakes failed and the car left the rails and smashed into a wall. Coping stones from the wall crashed through the windows and hit the seated passengers. Fifteen people were injured. The brakeman, Edward Harris, aged thirty-five, and a twelve-year-old girl, Margaret Worthington, were killed as they leapt from the tram. The company was wound up as a result of claims for damages. However, the tramway remained open and in 1948 the local council purchased the whole system. It remains a very popular tourist attraction. The picture above was taken very soon after the accident occurred.

CHAPTER FOUR

INTERNAL COMBUSTION ENGINE

The Swallow Falls Hotel in Betws-y-Coed, c. 1920. A variety of buses and cars are gathered in the early years of the development of North Wales as a major tourist centre.

The part that the internal combustion engine plays in our lives can never be underestimated. It is difficult for us to conceive of a world without motor cars, lorries etc. We curse them because of the environmental damage they cause through road building, gaseous pollution and the consumption of unrenewable energy sources, but we find it difficult to produce an alternative. It must be remembered that at the turn of the century, and into the 1920s, the motor car was a toy for the wealthy. Cars had to be built laboriously of hand-crafted components. The coachwork was designed and manufactured by craftsmen whose normal trade was building phaetons and landaus. One early car was designed with a whip holder for the driver — recognition of road rage perhaps. Cars impinged on the life of ordinary folks inasmuch as they frightened the horses, and pedestrians occasionally had to leap out of the way of men waving red flags. Above all, the early motor vehicles were unreliable, noisy and produced unbelievable amounts of dust and pollution on the world's unmetalled roads. The arrival of the taxi in about 1907 in London and the major conurbations caused riots among horse-drawn cab drivers, but now, at last, the man in the street could make use of the motor car. In 1908 the arrival of the Model T Ford changed all this, and that is where the trouble began.

On the forecourt of the 'Shell Motor Spirit Garage' at Llanrug near Caernarfon the owner is proudly displaying his fleet of vehicles, *c.* 1914. The open car on the left is a 12 hp Star, built in 1908 by the Star Engineering Co. of Wolverhampton. This company produced its first car in 1898 as a subsidiary to its cycle production, but stopped car production in 1932. The cars were extremely well made, well furnished and rather expensive. The other car is a 1908/9 Minerva built in Belgium. The company which produced it ceased car production in 1956. A notable feature on this car is the early use of electric headlights which were introduced around 1912. The motor cycle combination in the background, with its precarious passenger seat, is probably a 1906–9 NSU.

A special occasion at Northop in Flintshire. The beautiful motor car obviously belongs to a visiting dignitary though no information is available concerning the occasion. The registration number of the vehicle is AW, a Shropshire number. The car is a 1908 Belsize 14 hp, built by Belsize Motors Ltd, Manchester (1897–1925).

A scene in Gloddaeth Street, Llandudno. W.S. Williams was a milliner and draper whose premises were situated in Mostyn Street and Gloddaeth Street. The Mostyn Street shop was bought by Robert Clare Baxter, and is now called Clares, one of the few privately owned shops in Mostyn Street. The van is a commercial version of the Model T Ford of about 1920–2 with a coiled-spring front suspension, one of the many options that could be added to the mass-produced Model T.

The increasing popularity of the motor car is evident in this photograph of Criccieth in the 1930s. The vehicles are of familiar English manufacture – Rover, Morris and Austin 7. There is a mixture of London and Lancashire registration plates, a precursor of the onslaught of motor vehicles which nowadays pour into North Wales resorts throughout the holiday season.

Since there were few cars on the road in the early years, the need for traffic control was not paramount. Early photographs show vehicles travelling with a disregard for the things we take for granted, e.g. driving on the left. The car centre right in the above photograph of Rhyl Promenade is on the right-hand side of the road and turning right! Clearly the driver is not expecting to meet an oncoming vehicle. As the number of vehicles increased it became essential to institute some means of regulating the flow of traffic. An early speed limit of 10 mph is an example, following the era of the man with the red flag. A number of schemes came into being, including one-way traffic systems, traffic lights, manual controls by the police and various instruction signs. The car below, with a Caernarfonshire number plate (CC684), an Austin 12/4 made in the late 1920s, is only one example of too many of the vehicles which come to grief following a disregard for road conditions and traffic regulations.

In 1905 the LNWR brought into service its steam lorry from Holywell station. With a maximum speed of 5 mph it was a replacement for the horse-drawn vehicles which carried luggage and passengers to the town from the Chester and Holyhead Railway station approximately 1 mile away down a very steep gradient. A report on the facilities available between town and station in 1912 stated that at one time 'the vehicular connection with the station was an old white horse, a rickety four wheeler, and a driver that Dickens would have revelled in portraying'. The fare to the town was 4*d*. Below is the Llandudno station steam wagon in Church Walks, Llandudno.

The LNWR put on several bus services in North Wales, the first starting on 10 July 1905 with this Milnes–Daimler double decker in the railway's coaching livery of plum and milk. This ran from Mold through Northop, Flint, Oakenhalt Mill and Connah's Quay. A single decker (see below) operated in Holywell from the station to the town from 11 October 1905. In addition to passengers the buses carried mail and parcels. The Holywell service was terminated by the newly built rail link from Holywell Junction to the town on 1 July 1912. Bus services of this kind could also be found around the Conway Valley and Anglesey. During the First World War the bus chassis were commandeered by the War Office and the bodies were stored until the war ended.

The GWR company introduced its own buses to combat the fiercely competitive bus services run by private companies which were seriously affecting railway traffic. The first GWR service out of Corwen to Cerrigydrudion, pictured here, began in 1922, following the route of the railway line. The services were later extended to Betws-y-Coed and Swallow Falls. GWR services eventually spread all over the rural areas of North Wales, competing with the ever-expanding Crosville services.

Cambrian Railways operated a small bus fleet in the Nefyn–Pwllheli area, as seen here in *c.* 1915. The driver at the wheel of this bus (CC163) is Tom Jones, the first driver employed by Cambrian Railways. Mr Jones was killed on 5 October 1916 at Bodfaen Road when his bus went out of control and overturned. It could be argued that the railways were signing their own death warrants by introducing these convenient door-to-door bus services.

'Cariure Lleyn hen a diwedda' is written on the bottom left of this very early photograph of the Aberdaron bus. Roughly translated the quotation is 'Lleyn transport old and new'. Aberdaron is a small and relatively remote village on the Lleyn Peninsula and this excellent photograph, on a postcard published by Roberts, Post Office, shows the new bus outside the Ship Hotel. The occasion has caused quite a stir in the community with the inhabitants of the village coming out to be photographed with the newly arrived conveyance. The 'old' in the quotation presumably refers to the donkey and to the horse and cart in the background. It is difficult for us to comprehend the impact these small bus services had on the lives of people in remote rural areas; because of this bus the inhabitants of the village were able to make journeys to the places on the destination board, 'Pwllheli, Sarn and Aberdaron', more quickly, frequently and comfortably than ever before. Below, at a later date, people in Aberdaron have climbed on the racked roof of the bus, turning it into a double decker.

Outside the Vigour Inn, Cemaes Bay, Anglesey, *c.* 1913. The bus, registered EY313, is named 'Alma', a 30 hp Lacre chain-driven vehicle. A popular vehicle with summer visitors, it ran a regular service to Amlwch with a fare of 4½*d* each way. The bus was owned by the Cemaes Motor and General Agency.

A very rare photograph of the promenade at Rhyl in front of the famous 'Merrie Men', *c.* 1905. It shows a strange hybrid vehicle which purports to be 'Groves Bus'. This was a conversion of a ten-seater car which supposedly ran in Shrewsbury before 1899. The car/bus is offering rides at 6*d* a trip on solid wheeled tyres, over rough roads. The high price for such conditions suggests that motor vehicle rides must have been a great novelty at the time.

The Wrexham Tramway, which opened in 1876 as a horse-drawn service, changed to electric in 1903 and became Wrexham & District Electric Tramways Ltd. Ten years later a bus service was started which fed into the tramway system from outlying districts. One of its buses is seen above, and the presence of the lady conductor suggests this is a wartime photograph. By August 1914 the company owned sixteen buses. In the photograph below, this Daimler CC Saloon (FM614) was its first bus and standing by it in the bowler hat is A.A. Hawkins who stayed with the company until 1933. The GWR system became one of its main competitors and this forced the closure of the tramway on 31 March 1927. The GWR bus company later merged with the tramway and formed the Western Transport Co. Ltd in 1930. This company lasted only three years before being swallowed up by Crosville in 1933.

The square at Dwygyfylchi, near Penmaenmawr, in two views with a gap of several years between them. Dwygyfylchi was an important tourist centre at the foot of the scenic Sychnant Pass and close to the sandy beaches of the Penmaenmawr shore. The 'four in hands' had trouble with the steep mountain passes and the passengers had to disembark frequently to lighten the burden for the struggling horses. The greater horse-power of the Leyland Hackney carriages made this unnecessary.

The Royal Blue (Llandudno Coaching and Carriage Co. Ltd) developed from a horse-drawn coach and carriage company based at an Oxford Road depot in Llandudno. At one time the company owned 150 horses. Motor vehicles were introduced in 1918. The early buses were Thorneycroft, but it later used Dennis, SOS and Leyland stock. In 1923 the company carried 763,383 passengers and recorded fewer than 400,000 miles; six years later in 1929 it carried 7,444,053 passengers and recorded 2,824,688 miles. It was bought by Crosville in the 1930s and had 80 buses in its fleet at the time.

On 24 March 1956 the Llandudno and Colwyn Bay Electric Tramway Co. operated its last tram, and on 25 March the board of directors announced that the service would be converted to buses. There was now direct confrontation between the 'Red' buses and Crosville, a confrontation which had an inevitability about it. In 1961 the ailing small bus company accepted the offer of £40,000 for the goodwill of the business, no other assets being purchased. In this photograph we see the 'Red Bus' breakdown van at the Church Road depot, Rhos-on-Sea.

The Silver Motors Ltd was a company registered in 1914 to take over the affairs of Llandudno Automobile Touring Co. Ltd, which had been in business for only three years at the time. Using Llandudno as a centre, the firm organized tours around North Wales and was also connected to a Chester company called Chester Silver Motors Co. By 1930 the Llandudno business owned more than twenty-seven buses. In this photograph six of the Dennis buses are outside Deganwy station with a large touring group, c. 1920.

Bangor Blue buses in the square at Caernarfon, in front of the main post office. In April 1928 this business was purchased by the Llandudno Royal Blue Co. It had depots at Bangor, Beaumaris and Llangefni. The routes ranged from Caernarfon to Betws-y-Coed but principally various routes throughout Anglesey. The purchase of the company by the Royal Blue greatly extended its territory and scope. It owned eighty buses when it was purchased by Crosville in the 1930s.

A very early Brookes Brothers White Rose Co. double decker on the front at Rhyl. This company controlled a strategic section of North Wales and had a large depot at Denbigh as well as Rhyl. Joseph, Daniel and Thomas Brookes started the business in about 1900, operating 'four in hand' horse-drawn coaches. Motor vehicles were introduced in 1911. The first motor charabanc was a Lacre (DM472). In 1912 the fleet consisted of five more charabancs and two open-topped double-deck buses, all made by Leyland. A further depot was opened in Prestatyn. By 1930 it owned eighty-nine buses, coaches and charabancs, almost all manufactured by Leyland. It was taken over by Crosville in the 1930s.

The tourist venue of Dyserth with its well-known waterfall was an easy excursion ride from Rhyl. This evocative photograph is a postcard taken by a very talented North Wales photographer, Rae Pickard of Rhyl, whose photographs from the early decades of the century delight collectors with their clarity, detail and subject-matter. This postcard has been to America and back, and informs the recipient in New Jersey that the child in the pram is 'Geoffrey Howel's little boy'. The White Rose double decker is one of the two owned by the company.

A small family company set up to assemble and sell cars in Chester in 1906, run by the Crosland Taylors, was later to become the largest bus operator in North Wales and the north-west. Car making ceased in 1908 when it purchased a small troublesome Herald charabanc, which it ran from central Chester to Ellesmere Port. It was one of those vehicles, common at the time, which would rather go downhill than uphill. There were several years of, to say the least, indifferent progress until in 1929 the company was sold to the LMS Railway company. This was followed by the dissolution of the board, but Claude and James Crosland Taylor stayed as managerial employees. Claude died young in 1935 and James was appointed general manager, a position he held until 1959. The company expanded its fleet, routes and influence by buying up the many smaller companies existing during the 1930s, e.g. White Rose (Rhyl), and Llandudno's Royal Blue. In all it purchased or annexed some 120 small companies in the late 1920s and early 1930s, before being nationalized in 1948. The above photograph was taken at the Chester depot in about 1921, and the man in the light suit is said to be James Crosland Taylor. The buses, 61 and 62, were purchased in 1921 and were the first with the Leyland body. Below is an early double-decker vehicle in Mostyn Street, Llandudno, c. 1930.

A Crosville Daimler 29 (FM224) with a strange open-sided body in Trelawney Square, Flint. This area underwent rapid industrial expansion between the wars, with the manufacture of artificial fibres and paper its major industries. The steel industry of Shotton was within commuting distance. Bus companies derived a great deal of their revenue from the transport of workers to and from the industrial sites. At specified shift-changing times the streets were full of buses carrying workers. As a student, the author worked as a conductor from the Flint depot for two three-month periods during the busy holiday seasons of 1949–51.

Crosville double- and single-decked vehicles reminiscent of the vehicles common on the roads in the late 1940s and early 1950s.

Chapter Five

Standard Gauge
Railways

An unrebuilt LMS 'Royal Scot' Class 4–6–0 running through the station with the longest name-board in Great Britain, watched by a posed lady in traditional Welsh costume. This engine was introduced in about 1930 to the Chester and Holyhead Railway.

Narrow gauge railways existed in North Wales from 1801 (Penrhyn quarry railway) and later 1828 (Nantlle Railways), but standard gauge railways did not emerge as major means of transport until the 1840–5 period. The first standard gauge railway was the main line 'Irish Mail' route from Chester to Holyhead completed in 1850 with the opening of Stephenson's bridge across the Menai Strait. This made a tremendous difference to the journey times between London and Holyhead. By 1860 the 'Irish Mail' was leaving Euston at 7.30 in the morning and arriving at Holyhead at 2.05 in the afternoon, beating the fastest stagecoach time of 1836 by some twenty hours. Letters posted early in the morning in London were reaching their destination in Dublin that same evening. The railway also had a tremendous effect on the economic life of the area. Coastal North Wales experienced a boom in the tourism industry, and large-scale exploitation of the area's mineral wealth was also possible — hitherto, it had been restricted by the established narrow gauge system's link with the seaboard. Many small cross-country routes and branch lines were opened, but most were ruthlessly dispensed with by Beeching during the 1960s, an act of shortsighted vandalism which is becoming increasingly apparent as the need for integrated traffic systems and the tyranny of the internal combustion engine are recognized.

The Chester and Holyhead Railway Co. was the last to be attracted to Chester as a point of departure for its rail routes in the mid-nineteenth century. Stations for the Chester and Birkenhead, and Chester and Crewe, railways already existed in the city. With the Shrewsbury and Chester Railway Co. a new station was planned and built, opening in 1848. By 1890 the GWR and LNWR were planning an enlargement of the station, which was owned jointly by the LNWR/LMS and the GWR until the railways were nationalized.

Above, a Hughes–Fowler 'Crab' 2–6–0 departs from Chester General station with an SLS (Stephenson Locomotive Society) excursion train in the 1950s. Below, in front of the collonade which once supported the station roof (now demolished), an ex-GWR 28xx class 2–8–0 runs through Chester station with a freight train.

The LNWR station was opened at Connah's Quay on 1 September 1870 and was rebuilt and enlarged in 1906. There was a branch line to the dock which was used largely for the transportation of minerals from the mining area of Wrexham. The station was demolished in 1966. The cooling towers in the background belonged to Rockliffe Hall coal-fired power station. These have now been demolished and replaced by a high-tech gas-fired system. A new Dee bridge opened in March 1998.

Bagillt station was built in 1849 on the Chester to Holyhead line. The village itself did not always receive a good press, and a book about the rail route published in 1947 described it as 'the chief eyesore on the Dee'. There was a small port here from which minerals, principally metal ores, were exported. The station stood and served the community for almost 120 years, finally closing in 1966.

Holywell station was opened in May 1848. It was expanded periodically through the second half of the century when two platforms and a subway were added. The main buildings were designed by Francis Thompson. It changed its name to Holywell Junction on 1 July 1912 when the Holywell branch line and the new Holywell Town station opened.

The opening day of the Holywell Town station in 1912. There was a steep (1 in 27) gradient between Holywell Junction and the Town station. The line was a little over a mile in length with an intermediate stopping point at St Winifride's Halt. Small tank locos (2–4–2) pulled the train in the early days, and 2519 in the photograph is an example. The station closed in 1954 as a result of the competition from increasing bus services in the area.

The exterior of Rhyl station on a postcard posted in 1908. This station was of inestimable importance in the development of Rhyl as a holiday and tourism centre. In 1938 740,000 people were incoming passengers at Rhyl station, and of this number, 630,000 passengers arrived during the summer holiday season from the industrial areas of Lancashire, Yorkshire and the Midlands. This once thriving station, with its major facilities for the traveller and its substantial sidings, has undergone many changes over the years, with the cab canopy (above) and the main building surviving as a reminder of its more prosperous past.

The photograph below, posted in 1910, shows the glass-canopied platform with the once familiar W.H. Smith's bookstall on the right.

On the night of 17 August 1879 the swollen River Dulas caused the collapse of the railway viaduct above it; fortunately there was no traffic involved. The disruption caused the immediate transfer of mail traffic by road through Abergele to Colwyn station. Work began immediately on a temporary line, with a gradient of 1 in 23 at either end. The line was a single one and carried the traffic 14 ft above the river. It was opened on 24 August for freight, and the first passenger train crossed the following day. The main girders, rolled at Crewe, were ready by 29 August and, using electric light for the first time to facilitate all-night working, the line was reopened less than a month later on 14 September, a feat which included the building of six stone piers. Above, a train is on the temporary bridge on the left. The coaches are in use to house the many workmen involved. Below, the six stone piers can be seen in a photograph taken soon after the accident. The train is an LNWR Webb 'Problem' or 'Lady of the Lake', class 2–2–2, introduced in about 1870. The train may well be the 'Irish Mail' since these locomotives were used very successfully on this service.

This station was built in 1849 when it was known simply as 'Colwyn'. The name Colwyn Bay was adopted in 1876. As local development took place largely because of the influence of the railway and expanding tourism, improvements were completed on the station in 1885. In 1904 widening produced a four-track section to Llandudno Junction. A ballast pit near the station was turned into a goods yard which opened on 28 March 1904 (bottom left). Work was eventually completed in March 1908, and the platforms were lengthened in 1910. Since this photograph was taken, the goods yard has been replaced by a large shopping complex. The yard's services were moved to Llandudno Junction, as here in Colwyn Bay it stood in the way of the development of the A55 expressway.

The site of the former Mochdre and Pabo station (1889–1931). It has a particular historical significance because it was near here that the first water troughs ever used on the world's railways were placed in 1860. Such troughs allowed the speeding trains to pick up water without stopping. Problems with water supply led to their being moved to Aber (near Llanfairfechan) in 1871. This section of the line was relocated to allow for the building of the A55 expressway which runs parallel with the line to Llandudno Junction.

The first station at Llandudno Junction on the Conway Embankment opened in 1860. Before this the train for Llandudno and district had been handled at Conway station, with which there was a horse-carriage link. In 1863 a line was opened from Conway to Llanrwst and this was later extended to Betws-y-Coed (1868) and Blaenau Ffestiniog (1879). In 1897 a larger station was built with four through platforms and bays for the Llandudno trains. There was an engine shed for twelve engines.

The rapid development of Llandudno as a fashionable resort in the latter quarter of the nineteenth century led to 2 miles of carriage sidings being laid on the station approaches. The present station at Llandudno was built in 1891. Five platforms were built, with a long carriageway between platforms 2 and 3. Fifteen trains an hour could arrive during the busy holiday seasons in the 1940s. Despite the rising popularity of the motor car, about 40,000 passengers per week arrived by train.

The running of the railway through the town of Conway presented the engineers with several problems. The crossing of the River Conway was solved by the construction of Stephenson's Tubular Bridge, which runs parallel to Telford's Suspension Bridge. Both bridges were trial runs for the much bigger bridges of the same structure across the Menai Strait. The town walls had to be cut circumspectly in order to conform with regulations. The original station at Conway was designed by Francis Thompson, but this was destroyed by fire in 1858. After rebuilding, it was made bigger on two subsequent reconstructions (1860 and 1875). The station closed in February 1966, and a new station was built in 1987. In this photograph the Down 'Irish Mail' is leaving the Tubular Bridge, c. 1910.

Penmaenmawr station was built in 1849. Two aspects of the town's character have determined the type of rail traffic it has received. One is the huge granite quarrying industry that dominates the landscape, with the massive hulk of Penmaenmawr ever present, and the other is its identity as a seaside resort. Extensive rail linkages and interchange facilities can be seen in the above photograph taken in the 1930s.

Bangor station is situated, and tightly squeezed, between the Bangor and Belmont tunnels. The Chester to Bangor stretch of the Chester and Holyhead Railway is 59¾ miles long and opened to passengers in May 1848. Bangor station was the terminus of the line for almost two years while the construction of the Britannia Tubular Bridge was being completed. The first station was designed by Francis Thompson. Much rebuilding went on to make the most of the space between the two tunnels. In the 1920s a major reconstruction programme was undertaken to enlarge the busy station. Above, the original Thompson building, and, below, the LMS enlargements implemented in 1927.

Rival claims for the Irish packet service had been made early in the nineteenth century by Porthdynllaen on the Lleyn Peninsula and by Ormeshead (Llandudno), but Holyhead received the backing of the government. There was a flurry of building and civil engineering projects on this north-eastern tip of Holyhead Island in the second half of the century. A temporary station was built in 1848, and a harbour of refuge was constructed which was almost 1½ miles long. For more than thirty years extensions and improvements were carried out. A new station, hotel, and harbour were opened officially on 17 June 1880 by HRH the Prince of Wales (later Edward VII). The hotel was a large five-storey building with platforms on each side of the inner harbour to facilitate transfer from train to steamer and vice versa. The hotel stood for almost a century before being demolished in 1979. It had been empty since its closure in 1951. Below, the departure of the boat express from Holyhead.

Prestatyn and Dyserth Railway. This line had its origins in the transport of minerals. In 1869 the 2¾ mile line was opened to link Prestatyn, Meliden and Dyserth. In the early days there were no passenger facilities, the line being used solely for the transport of limestone and various mineral ores, such as lead, zinc, silver, copper and iron, which formed the basis for the industries in the area. Before the construction of the railway, mine products were transported by horse and cart on very poor road surfaces to the main lines, or went to the small port of Rhuddlan nearby.

In response to public demand, passenger services were started on 28 August 1905 when Railmotor No. 1 carried civic dignitaries to lunch in the Dyserth goods yard. The line existed for many years but the last passenger train ran on 20 September 1930 and slowly thereafter the freight traffic declined, leaving only a single stone and lime train each day from 1963. This ceased altogether in 1973.

This picture dates from shortly after the inaugural journey in 1905 at Prestatyn main line station. The Chester and Holyhead Rail tracks are on the right. The train is Railmaster No. 1. The railmaster was a self-contained vehicle with a non-detachable steam engine driving one of the bogies and operated by a two-man crew. This type of vehicle was used in the passenger service until they were replaced by conventional loco stock just before the line was closed to passengers in 1930.

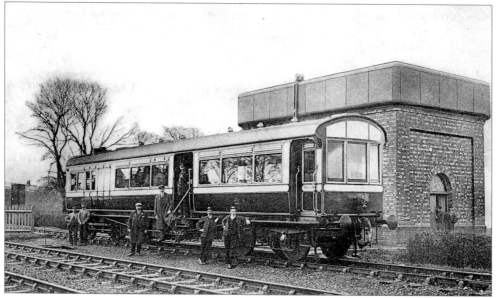

A clearer view of car No. 1 at Prestatyn station, c. 1905. The modern diesel car has much in common with the railmotor: the steam engine was at one end, separated from the passenger compartments by a luggage bay. The railmotors could be driven from either end. They were built by the LNWR and the railway had seven of them. The two compartments on either side of the central entrance were either smoking or non-smoking, each holding twenty-four passengers on rushwork seats.

A general view of the Prestatyn–Dyserth line, *c.* 1920. Meliden station is just off the bottom left of this photograph. There is a small goods yard to the right of the station. The light areas in the middle distance are the waste tips of the Talargoch lead mine, said to have been started by the Romans. There are no signs of the mining activities visible today, and the waste tips have gone. This photograph was taken from an area where there was a short-lived quarry called Craig Fawr.

Rhuddlan Road station, 1910. The railmotor is No. 4 which arrived in 1906 in the second batch of rolling stock. The platform sports a small waiting room, but the facilities for passengers at the small halts were very limited. All activity ceased on the line in 1973 and seven years later the tack was removed and the area has reverted to nature. It is as if it had never been.

CHAPTER SIX

NARROW GAUGE RAILWAYS

Welsh Pony, *the fifth engine to be built for the Ffestiniog Railway in 1867. After its boiler was condemned in 1938 the 0–4–0 engine was withdrawn and is now on display on a plinth outside Harbour station. One of the major tourist attractions in Wales, the Ffestiniog Railway, began its long life (over 150 years to date) as a horse-operated tramway carrying slates from the Blaenau Ffestiniog quarries to the port of Porthmadog. The line was constructed to take advantage of a falling gradient from quarry to port. Full wagons were gravity motivated and then drawn back to the quarry by horses. The horses were carried back to Porthmadog in 'dandy waggons'. Steam haulage arrived in 1863 when the first engines built by George England of New Cross, London, were introduced. More powerful engines were required and in 1869 the world-renowned 'Fairlies' made their appearance. The* Little Wonder *was the first of the 'double enders' with a central firebox. Over the years 300 Fairlies were built, both standard and narrow gauge, and they served in railways all over the world.*

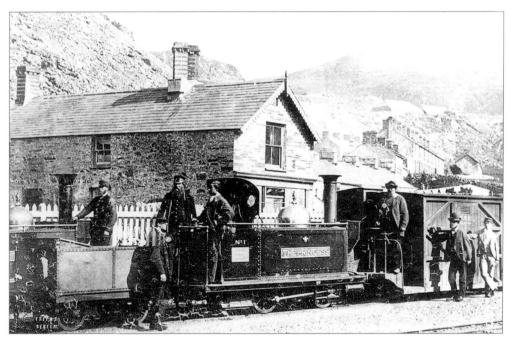

A very early view of the Ffestiniog Railway and the historic *Princess*. This was the first steam locomotive in the world for a public narrow gauge railway and the first steam locomotive on the Ffestiniog Railway, arriving in August 1863. It has been exhibited widely in various steam railway celebrations and entered the Ffestiniog Railway Museum in 1981.

Double 'Fairlie' engines are a well-known feature of the Ffestiniog Railway. They were introduced to the line in 1869. The first, *Little Wonder*, was followed by *James Spooner* in 1872, *Merddin Emrys* in 1879, and in 1885 by this engine, the *Livingston Thompson*. Seen here in about 1900 the engine has been much rebuilt over the years since then. It was later renamed *The Taliesin* and in 1961 it became *The Earl of Merioneth*.

This very early postcard view shows the high-level timber viaduct which carried slate wagons across the LNWR line to the dressing mills. The wooden structures had to be replaced several times in the interests of safety during the lifetime of the viaduct. At the lower level the narrow gauge lines ran to the Ffestiniog Railway depot at Dinas. The house and surrounding open space were eventually swamped by slate waste.

A view of Duffws station, *c.* 1905. This was the eastern terminus of the Ffestiniog Railway. *James Spooner* with assembled crew 'poses' for the photographer. The slate mountains in the background still tower over Blaenau Ffestiniog. Passenger traffic ceased at this station in 1931 and the area was used as a marshalling yard for slate trains. It is now a car park.

Two passenger trains at the Tan-y-Bwlch station, *c.* 1875. *James Spooner* is on the left. Built in 1872 by Avonside, it was the second double 'Fairlie' to be built. The empty middle line was removed in 1896.

A scene at Porthmadog, *c.* 1920. Standing by *Palmerston* are two brothers named Davies and the person behind them is Mr Robert Evans, the manager of the railway at this time. *Palmerston* came to Ffestiniog in 1863 and was rebuilt in 1888. It was the first engine built by England to have an enclosed cab. For many years from 1923 it worked on the Welsh Highland Railway as well as the Ffestiniog line. In 1974 it was sold to the Palmerston Locomotive Group for restoration. In the photograph a 'Fairlie' locomotive is backing on to the train for the return journey to Blaenau Ffestiniog.

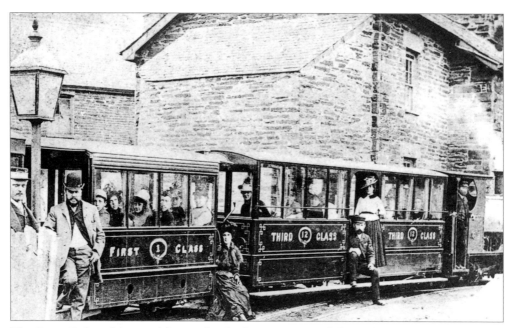

The Corris Railway began its life as a slate haulage tramway with horse-drawn carriages linking the quarry with the nearest navigable waterway, the River Dovey, with a quay at Derwenlas. It had a gauge of 2 ft 3 in and was opened in 1859. Steam locomotives were introduced in 1879, and a passenger service began in 1883. Five years after the opening a standard gauge Cambrian Railways line arrived, which passed through Machynlleth. The Corris line was never a wealthy line, serving as it did a very rural community. The loss of the slate industry led to its neglect, and eventually it was sold to the GWR for the princely sum of £1,000! The GWR immediately scrapped the uneconomic passenger service and started a minimal freight service. A flooded River Dovey wreaked havoc in 1948 and the line closed. Two locos and some other stock were sold to the Tal-y-Llyn Railway in 1951. The photograph below shows Llwyngwern station, *c.* 1902. The line on the bottom right is a short branch to Llwyngwern slate quarry which is now the site of the National Centre for Alternative Technology.

Vale of Rheidol Light Railway. In 1896 a bill was passed to construct a narrow gauge railway through the beautiful Rheidol Valley from Devil's Bridge to Aberystwyth. Five years later work began, and the line was completed in 1902. Freight traffic began in August 1902 and passenger traffic in December 1902. The lead mining industry provided the freight, and forestry work also utilized the line. The local farmers and miners were the original passengers. The developing holiday industry in Wales prompted the owners to try to attract trade in that quarter. Passing from owner to owner, the railway has, for most of its life, been solely a tourist attraction. The demise of the lead mining industry and the increasing domination of local passenger traffic by bus services meant that the line would have closed without tourism.

POST CARD.

THIS SPACE FOR COMMUNICATION
INLAND POSTAGE ONLY.

ADDRESS ONLY.

Inland
1/2 d

Foreign
1 d

EXCLUSIVE PHOTO COLOR SERIES
PUBLISHED BY THE PHOTOCHROM C o. LONDON.
Printed in England

THE BEST, PRETTIEST, AND CHEAPEST
WAY OF VISITING THE
DEVIL'S BRIDGE
IS BY THE
Vale of Rheidol Light Railway
(GAUGE, 1 FT. 11½ IN.)

The Scenery along the route is unrivalled for beauty and grandeur. It was first disclosed to view by the Railway and is still only seen from the trains. No visitor to Aberystwyth should miss this excursion.

Devil's Bridge station on the Vale of Rheidol Light Railway, 1903. The station is only a short distance from Pont-ar-Fynach (Devil's Bridge). A deep ravine with attendant waterfalls provides spectacular views from Jacob's Ladder, a flight of over 100 steps.

Aberystwyth station, Vale of Rheidol Light Railway, c. 1910. The company started its life as an independent concern in 1902, was taken over by the Cambrian Railways in 1910 and merged with the GWR in 1922. It was nationalized in 1948 and returned to the private sector in 1988.

The Glyn Valley Tramway was built to carry slate and stone from the quarries above Glyn Ceiriog to the Shropshire Union Canal near Chirk. The tramway was designed for horse-drawn vehicles in its early years. It opened in 1873 for freight traffic, and for passenger traffic in 1874. In 1888 the line was converted to steam and among the locomotives purchased was *Sir Theodore*, shown here in the yard at Chirk, *c.* 1911. From left to right: Elias Morris (platelayer), -?-, R. Jones, J. Morris and J. Roberts.

Most of the freight tonnage was stone and slate, but the train also carried wool, flannel and silica. In 1913 company records show that it carried 60,000 tons of stone for tramway footings, paving stones and macadam chippings. In the same year over 40,000 third class passengers were carried. The line was eventually extended to join up with the GWR line at Chirk. After the First World War the demand for granite declined and so did the fortunes of the tramway. Passenger services ceased in 1933 and the line eventually closed to traffic in 1935. After closure the track was lifted and transferred to Gresford to be used in the new workings opened up to replace those lost after the appalling pit disaster of 22 September 1934, when 262 miners and 3 rescuers lost their lives.

Sir Theodore at Glyn Ceiriog station on a postcard sent in 1905. The engine is named after Sir Theodore Martin, who was a director of the company, and who was said to have invested over £20,000 in it, a vast sum in those days. The engine cost £1,200. In 1889 *Dennis* was purchased, named after Henry Dennis who was the engineer and a director of the company. In 1892 a third locomotive, *Glyn*, was bought.

Glyn and *Dennis* outside the loco shed at Chirk, *c.* 1895. In the cab of *Glyn*, in the foreground, are James Roberts and James Hughes. Standing beside *Dennis* are John Morgan and John Williams. The names of the other men are unknown.

Talyllyn Railway. A posed publicity photograph for the Talyllyn Railway (above) used as a postcard and published by Valentine, *c*. 1924. The train is the *Talyllyn* and it has stopped at Pentremaestrefnant approaching the Abergynolwen terminus. It is part of the passenger service and is being driven by William Lewis.

Built to transport slate from the Nant Gwernol Valley at Abergynolwen and Dolgoch, the Talyllyn Railway was the first to attract a band of dedicated supporters who formed a preservation society after the death of Sir Haydn Jones in 1950. The Talyllyn reopened for business in 1951. The line had been opened in 1866 and was about 10 miles long, running to the wharf close to the Cambrian Railways line at Towyn. It was a 2 ft 3 in gauge line, thus wider than the Ffestiniog but the same gauge as the Corris line with which there was an operational link.

Rolling stock has been carefully preserved and is in remarkably good condition considering that much of it is over 100 years old. Stock purchased from defunct lines has been used to boost the existing stock. The two original engines were the *Dolgoch* and the *Talyllyn*, built by Fletcher Jennings and Co. of Whitehaven. Later *Sir Haydn* and *Edward Thomas* were purchased from the Corris Railway.

Nantmoor station (above) on the Welsh Highland Railway. The Welsh Highland Railway system was completed in 1923 and, after a short and relatively unhappy life, it closed in 1937. Initially there had been great hopes of its viability as a tourist attraction. The railway came into being by joining several existing narrow gauge lines until eventually it was possible to travel from Dinas to Porthmadog and then from Porthmadog to Blaenau Ffestiniog. Declining industrial traffic and increasing bus services led to a decrease in demand for the service and a receiver was appointed in 1927. The following six years saw no improvement so the line was closed. It was reopened briefly by the Ffestiniog Railway Co. with little success, and in 1937 it was decided not to operate the line any longer. During the war much of the track and artefacts were requisitioned to aid the war effort. A preservation society is currently making commendable efforts to revitalize the system. Rhyd-Ddu, South Snowdon station (below), has rather a misleading name since the station is a few miles from Snowdon. However, the company's literature described an excursion from the station as 'the shortest and most picturesque route to Snowdon' in an attempt to attract the tourist trade.

Space precludes a comprehensive survey of all of the quarry engines working in North Wales in the latter half of the last century and into this century. The subject demands a separate volume. Therefore, only a few examples can be considered here. Narrow gauge in Wales started with a 2 ft gauge line from Lord Penrhyn's slate quarry to Port Penrhyn at Bangor as early as 1801, when the pulling power was supplied by horses. In 1879 a new railway was built for steam locomotive haulage. *Blanche* with her sister *Linda* arrived in 1893 and is seen here in a very early photograph shortly after her arrival. The photograph below shows *Blanche* at work in Port Penrhyn in 1947. In 1963 she was purchased by the Ffestiniog Railway and was rebuilt in 1972.

No. 1 shunts near the slate mills at Hafod Owen, Dinorwic. This Hunslet saddletank was acquired by the Dinorwic quarry in 1922 and worked as a shunter at Port Dinorwic before going to the quarry. To facilitate quarry work the cab was removed, the chimney shortened and the sprung bumpers replaced by side dumb blocks. In 1967 No. 1 was sold for restoration and preservation in Hampshire.

The third level of the Penrhyn quarry, *c*. 1947. The engine is *Glyder* in this excellent photograph of a working train.

The Fairbourne Miniature Railway started life as a horse-drawn tramway on a 2 ft gauge to transport building materials from Fairbourne brickworks to Penrhyn Point across the Mawddach estuary from Barmouth. When building ceased a horse-drawn passenger service began. In 1916 the character of the tramway changed: steam traction was introduced, and the gauge changed to 1 ft 3 in. During the Second World War the line stopped functioning and fell into dereliction, but thereafter a group of businessmen bought it and revitalized it.

Rhyl Miniature Railway had a 1 ft 3 in gauge and was the longest established line with this gauge in Great Britain. The line provided a run of almost a mile around the Marine Lake Amusement Park. The railway started its life in 1911, at a time when the resort of Rhyl was becoming one of the premier holiday venues of the North Wales coast. The locomotives were built by W. J. Bassett-Lowke of Northampton who, with Henry Greeling as engineer, established the system. The photograph above was probably taken in the year of its opening. The very busy line worked every day of the week during the summer season, working from early morning to late evening on a fifteen-hour day. The route was a circular one around the picturesque lake so the passengers were able to face the engine for the whole of the ride. After the line closed one of the engines was displayed at the Railway Museum at Tyseley, Birmingham.

Snowdon Mountain Railway. The initial proposal to run a railway line to the summit of Snowdon met with considerable opposition, not least from the owner of the mountain, Mr W.A. Assheton Smith. He could see no benefit accruing from such a venture for the people of Llanberis, and the result would be a dreadful scar on the landscape. The rivalry between Llanberis and Beddgelert for the prime tourist position eventually persuaded Mr Assheton Smith, and in 1894 the Snowdon Mountain Tramroad and Hotels Co. was formed. Work began on the two viaducts required for the system on 15 December 1894. The track was laid at a phenomenal rate of 120 yd per day, but the working conditions during the winter were appalling. Masons were paid 8*d* per hour and labourers 5*d*, with a height money bonus of 2*d* and 1*d* respectively. At the end of the day the men slept where their day's work had finished.

The railway officially opened on Easter Monday 1896, but there was a fatal accident on the inaugural journey (see p. 89). This led to the line being closed for a year. After re-opening it carried 12,000 passengers to the summit in a year. Below, a Royal Blue motor coach from Llandudno has carried tourists to Llanberis station for their trip to Snowdon summit.

Early travellers at the summit accompanied by the obligatory guides, late nineteenth century. The crinolined ladies would have made heavy weather of the walk up; they were probably carried on horseback. The summit with its huge cairn was a clutter of unsightly huts at this time. Tourist interest in Snowdonia was aroused following the opening of the Chester and Holyhead Railway in 1848 with its station at Bangor. A branch line was opened to Caernarfon in 1852 and to Llanberis in 1869.

On the day of the official opening, train No. 1 *Ladas* (the initial letters of Laura Alice Duff Assheton Smith) left the track just above Clogwyn station and plunged down a ravine. The crew jumped clear. Two passengers defied orders to stay put and leapt from the train – one of them died from injuries received. The line was closed for a year so that appropriate safety modifications could be made.

The track design for the Abt system of traction. The distance between each and every tooth is exactly the same, so that the train's pinion is always in contact with the track below. The whole 5-mile track (approx.) was laid from Llanberis to the summit in seventy-two working days – an amazing feat when one considers the relatively primitive working tools used and the prevailing winter conditions.

The upper viaduct with two-coach train, *c*. 1905. The absence of smoke signifies that the train is descending. The coaches are pushed up the mountain by the train and held in check by the train when it is coming down as the motive power on descent is gravity. The two viaducts over the River Hwch were built by Chambers of Manchester and were the first construction work on the railway, since all future work depended upon their completion. They were built in the winter months of 1894–5 so that track could be laid in 1895. The lower viaduct is 166 yd long, and the upper is 63 yd long with each arch 4 ft higher than the one preceding it.

Locomotive No. 2 *Enid* was one of the first batch of locomotives built in Winterthur, Switzerland. It cost £1,525. *Ladas*, purchased at the same time, was destroyed on the first official journey on the opening day. *Enid* was named after Mr Assheton Smith's daughter. This engine was the original 'work horse' on the system, carrying machinery and rail parts during the construction of the railway. It is the oldest engine associated with the Snowdon Mountain Railway.

Clogwyn station, *c.* 1910. The semaphore signalling system seen here was used as traffic control in the early years. Five locos operated the system and this is No. 4 *Snowdon* waiting until the descending train has passed. *Snowdon* arrived at Llanberis on 23 August. It was taken out of the system early in the history of the railway, but in 1961 it was rebuilt at Leeds and returned.

This later photograph of Clogwyn station is after the removal of the old semaphore signalling system in 1930. Men stationed at the passing loops on the system issued tickets of 'authorization' and there was a telephone communication system. The train shown here is No. 5 *Moel Siabod*, named after one of the mountains in the range. *Moel Siabod* arrived at Llanberis at the end of 1897. The coach was one built by the Societé Industrielle Suisse, Neuhaven, and is one of those which started service during 1921–2.

The summit station, *c.* 1910. The hotel is on the summit in this photograph, and this unsightly cluster of buildings was there until the early 1930s. The station facilities shown here were for the exclusive use of the railway staff until the building of the new station and hotel complex (designed by Clough Williams-Ellis of Port Meirion fame). The hotel veranda was used by visitors to watch the spectacular sunrises for which the area is famed.

CHAPTER SEVEN

PORTS & HARBOURS

Up until the eighteenth century the Dee was the point of departure for very many voyages to Ireland and London. The shifting sands of the Dee have, over the centuries, presented many problems. Connah's Quay docks were built by the Wrexham, Mold and Connah's Quay Railway Co. in the latter half of the nineteenth century. This quay was instrumental in the movement of materials for the adjacent steel works, coal mines and brickworks of the Wrexham, Mold and Buckley area. The line to the quay linked with the Chester and Holyhead Railway at Connah's Quay station. Shipbuilding was an important activity at the turn of the century and continued up to the 1930s. The maritime families of Connah's Quay included Coppack, Vickers, Bennet, Reney, Hughes, Bithel, Foulkes, Parry and Roberts. Ferguson & Baird and J. Crichton were the main shipbuilders.

Summers' steelworks harbour, *c.* 1920. A fleet of ships driven by the internal combustion engine sailed from this harbour from approximately 1910 to 1947. Boats built mainly by local builders predominated until the fleet reached twenty-one in number. The boats had distinctive names: *Carita, Fleurita, Indorita, Eldorite, Warita*, etc. They carried pig iron from Lancashire mills and slag (a fertilizer by-product of the smelting process) was carried to Scotland and Ireland. Steel sheets were carried for transfer to larger ships at Birkenhead and Liverpool.

Coastal trading vessels at Bagillt, *c.* 1880–90. The Bagillt gully has been a small fishing port for centuries. Mining and industrial development in the eighteenth century saw the development of a small port here. Lead and other minerals were carried by small boats to larger craft waiting at Parkgate on the Wirral Peninsula. There was further development of the port in the nineteenth century until the railways began to take over. In its heyday as a port it was visited by paddle steamers carrying passengers from Liverpool and the Wirral. On these day trips the boats were met by horse-drawn carriages to Holywell, Flint, Denbigh and St Asaph. These packet services came to an end around 1895 when the Wrexham–Liverpool train service began to operate.

Two Mersey 'flats' moored at the quayside at Mostyn in the Dee estuary at the turn of the century. The right-hand boat, *The Temple*, was, by the evidence of her funnel, a 'sailing steamer'. There has been a dock at Mostyn for centuries, and because of the promontory called 'The Tip' and the use of flushing reservoirs to disperse the natural silting that occurs Mostyn dock is the only working one left on the Dee estuary.

The first steamers to arrive at Rhyl landed their cargoes and passengers on the beach with the help of local fishermen who provided the ferrying. In 1831 demands from regular steamer sailings led to the building of a small pier at the Foryd. Grain and agricultural produce were transported as well as passengers. The absence of a railway until 1848 and the dreadful conditions on the roads made the harbour the principal entry point to the town for the burgeoning tourist trade. A regular packet service was established between Rhuddlan and Liverpool from 1831, which called at Foryd harbour. Over the years over thirty ships were built in the vicinity of the harbour, all of them sailing ships, some fully rigged.

Port Penrhyn, Bangor, *c.* 1910. This slate port was built in 1790 and enlarged in 1800 to accommodate fifty ships. It was built by Pennant, the owner of the Penrhyn slate quarry. A narrow gauge tramway was built between the quarry and the port in 1801. In 1852 the port was linked with the Chester and Holyhead Railway and consequently there was a mixture of standard and narrow gauge lines at the port. Slate was off-loaded from narrow gauge to standard gauge rail or directly to ships.

An early photograph of Port Dinorwic (Y Felinheli) which shows it in its glory days functioning as the main export point for slate from the Dinorwic quarries. This was the harbour of the Menai Strait linked by tramway to Mr Assheton Smith's quarry 7 miles inland to the south-east. A tramway was built to this area in 1824 and this was improved by a rail link built in 1840–2. From this port large quantities of slate were carried to destinations as far away as Australia and the West Indies.

The port of Beaumaris, which acquired its name in the reign of Edward I, was of particular importance early in the maritime history of North Wales. Known as Gwyg Yr, it was a port of great significance. In 1701 it was credited with a single ship of only 14 tons, but by the end of the eighteenth century it boasted 300 vessels with a tonnage of nearly 14,000. By the end of the Napoleonic wars the figure had almost doubled to 538 ships with a tonnage of 25,000 tons. There was a thriving shipbuilding industry at Beaumaris at this time. Then fortunes changed, and the port's rivals, such as Caernarfon, bolstered by the slate industry, and Barmouth with its wool exports, began to overtake and surpass Beaumaris in importance. The Dee estuary was also a busy shipping area and the port of Chester became the pre-eminent north-western port.

A technically superb photograph of the port of Amlwch, Anglesey, c. 1908. The port has witnessed two flurries of activity in its history. One was the discovery of copper at nearby Parys Mountain (Mynydd Parys) at the end of the last century. The mine became one of the largest copper mines in the world, and the port boomed as the export point for copper ore to smelters in Lancashire and Swansea. The industry declined and by 1914 the harbour was very quiet. A second boom occurred around 1970 when it became the terminal for an off-shore oil company. This operation ceased in 1987.

Holyhead breakwater, photographed here in 1908, has provided respite for sailors from the angry storms of the Irish Sea since 1873. It protects the Holyhead outer harbour and, at 1.86 miles long, is the longest in Great Britain. Seven million tons of stone were quarried from Holyhead Mountain and used in its construction. It took upwards of 1,000 men 28 years to build the structure. Work began in 1845 and it was completed in 1873, when it was declared open by Albert Edward, Prince of Wales in August of that year. It cost £1,285,000. The Z-shape came about as a result of an initial design fault being rectified part way through the construction.

Caernarfon was the main port for the Dyffryn Nantlle slate quarries and photographs of the Slate quay show the serried ranks of slates waiting to be transported to port all over Europe and, occasionally, to North America. This trade was very important to the town in the early years of this century, and photographs of the time always show a large number of vessels waiting to be loaded.

Pwllheli was the major port of the Lleyn Peninsular for centuries. A pier was built here in the reign of George III. In 1903 an inner harbour was constructed but was seldom used because of excessive silting. It was a thriving shipbuilding area. Between 1759 and 1878 over 460 ships were built in the area, many of them over 600 tons which was large for this time. By 1901 only about 100 ships a year frequented the port, largely importing coal and general goods and exporting agricultural produce. Land reclamation led to channel changes and increased silting. Quarry waste was discharged at the harbour mouth, which further diminished the port's viability, while improved road and rail facilities accelerated the inevitable demise of the port.

PORTMADOC HARBOUR 1878.

Porthmadog grew up in the 1820s alongside the massive embankment built by Alexander Madocks of Tremadoc to reclaim 2,000 acres of land at the mouth of the River Glaslyn. The port's function was primarily to export slate from the Ffestiniog quarries. Around 1862 114,000 tons of slate were being exported annually. The town was linked to the quarries by the world-famous Ffestiniog narrow gauge railway. Standard gauge rail seriously diminished sea-going trade and by 1890 50 per cent of local slate was carried by rail. Porthmadog remained a busy port and was also an important shipbuilding centre. It became famous for its three-masted schooners for the Newfoundland trade. Designed by David Jones and built by him, David Williams and Ebenezer Roberts, they were the equal of any ship in the world carrying sail. Shipbuilding continued to be a profitable industry until the First World War. The last to be built, *Gestiana*, launched in 1913, was lost on her maiden voyage to Newfoundland, which was a crippling financial loss for Porthmadog shipbuilding.

Barmouth was the principal port of Merioneth and during the eighteenth and early nineteenth century was home to a rich maritime life. In its early years the main export trade was Welsh wool, but later Barmouth harbour played a significant part in the Caernarfon slate trade along with Caernarfon, Bangor and Port Dinorwic. The harbour also provided an invaluable local amenity for carrying goods and commodities to the smaller communities served by the River Mawddach as far as Dolgellau. When Porthmadog harbour was completed in 1824 an implicit partnership was established between Barmouth and Porthmadog, continuing until the decline of the slate trade, which dealt a severe blow to all the ports of Caernarfonshire and Merioneth.

The small port of Aberdyfi was rebuilt in 1868 in order to cope with a worldwide demand for Welsh roofing slate. The Cambrian Railways was responsible for the reconstruction. It attempted to institute a packet service to Ireland from the port in opposition to Holyhead, but the venture met with little success. Again, the decline of the slate industry led to the demise of the port.

CHAPTER EIGHT

WRECKS & LIFEBOATS

The launch of the Rhyl lifeboat, c. 1910. The main shipping routes into the north-west and into Ireland all pass close to the rugged North Wales coastline. Daily, dozens of vessels moved in and out of the ports of Liverpool, Holyhead, Chester and the Dee estuary. The vagaries of nature, ill judgement and ill luck all too frequently combined to draw vessels into disaster on the deadly stretches of coast which make up Anglesey and the Lleyn Peninsula. Between 1800 and 1850 1,000 people were drowned within sight of Llandudno and many more around the northern coasts into Cardigan Bay. This chapter presents photographs of shipwrecks and also of lifeboats manned by volunteer heroes. Nowhere is man's humanity to man more clearly seen than in the lives of the hundreds of lifeboatmen who risk all with little regard for themselves. The National Institution for the Preservation of Life from Shipwrecks came into being in 1824, the first organized national structure to deal with the daily disasters that struck around Britain's shores. In 1854 it changed its name to the Royal National Lifeboat Institution and a string of lifeboats and lifeboat houses sprang up around Britain's coasts, each manned by volunteer crews of exemplary courage.

One of the world's first self-propelled submersibles, the *Resurgam*. In 1879 the Revd W.D. Garrett took delivery of this now famous product of his genius. The craft had been built to his specifications by Messrs Cochrain's boiler manufacturers of Birkenhead. Garrett speedily fitted her out and with his crew took her out of the Mersey and on to the waters off Rhyl. His submersion trials were completely successful and after eleven weeks he arranged for the Admiralty to submit her for further trials with a view to her adoption and development by the Royal Navy. He left Rhyl under tow by the steam yacht *Elfin* for Portsmouth. That same night in February disaster overtook the submarine and she is believed to have broken away from her tow craft. The events of the night are not at all clear. Apparently the towing yacht's engines failed and as the sea was rough and choppy with gale force winds it is conceivable that the yacht had to sever its towing cables. The submarine was never seen again. The *Elfin* was spotted the following day and the *Fire King*, a tug owned by Coppacks of Connah's Quay, went to her aid. Unfortunately the *Elfin* was rammed by the tug and she quickly sank. The wreck of the *Resurgam* has been found recently (1997) and funds are being sought for her raising.

An abortive attempt to help the war effort in 1916. This is a rare photograph of a wreck which occurred on the rocks near Bull Bay, Amlwch, Anglesey. The boat is the Mersey ferry, *Pansy*, which was built in 1896 for the Wallasey Corporation. With a gross capacity of 333 tons, the *Pansy* was 180 ft long. She was requisitioned for war service, and it was when she was on her way to London that disaster struck.

In Liverpool Bay, 15 miles east of Llandudno, one of the great sea tragedies occurred on Thursday 1 June 1939. With a crew of fifty-five on board, the *Thetis* left Cammell Laird's yard, Birkenhead, for sea trials. There were also an additional fifty dockyard technicians aboard. She failed to surface after her first dive – water had flooded through a torpedo tube into her forward compartments. Four men escaped using Davis' apparatus. For a while her stern appeared, but soon she slid beneath the waters. Five months after the dreadful tragedy, because war had been declared and there was a desperate need for submarines, she was dragged to Traeth Bychan beach near Moelfre, Anglesey. There she was drained and cleared. With the bodies removed and repairs effected, the vessel was renamed the *Thunderer* and went into service. She was eventually sunk in 1943 off Sicily.

The Point of Ayr lifeboat, *H.G. Powell*, photographed at Llanasa on 5 June 1896. Point of Ayr is on the Dee estuary with its treacherous shifting sands and swirling tides. The boat was built in 1895 and cost £1,500. The crew and the boat's supporters are photographed here. Twelve oarsmen provided the power for the boat's propulsion.

There were three consecutive lifeboats at Rhyl, all based on the same design – two parallel banana-shaped tubular floats joined at each end with open slatted gratings in between. They were affectionately known as the 'banana' boats. The design, by Richardson of Bala, was very stable but the water splashed up through the gratings and the crew were very exposed. The first of these boats arrived in 1856 and their most famous rescue was in the great storm of 1859 when they saved the lives of five men and a boy from the schooner *Oriental*. *Morgan* served for thirty-seven years before being scrapped in 1893. *Caroline Richardson* lasted four years to 1897 and was broken up in 1899. Pictured here is *Caroline Richardson II*, which served forty-two years at Rhyl and was withdrawn in 1939.

The Abergele lifeboat was transferred to Llanddulas in 1869 after only a year. A boathouse was built on the shore, paid for by R. Bamford Hesketh of Gwyrch Castle. The lifeboat, the *Henry Nixon*, had to wait for seven years before its first rescue. It was taken out of service in 1885 and replaced by the *Mary Jane Gould*. In operation the boat was hauled over the shingle by three pairs of horses, as seen here. There was little call for the service of the *Mary Jane Gould* and she was withdrawn in 1909, to be replaced by the *Brother and Sister*. The station was closed in 1932 after sixty-four years, during which time the lifeboat was launched fifteen times with eight effective rescues, saving, in all, twenty-one lives.

There has been long history of lifeboat activity at Llandudno. The bay, with its two prominent limestone headlands close to the busy Mersey and Dee shipping lanes, seems to have attracted more than its share of shipping disasters. On 3 August 1900 after a fierce storm fifty sailing boats were wrecked in Llandudno Bay in one night! The first lifeboat was the *Sister's Memorial* (1861–7). The *Theodore Price*, pictured here, arrived in 1902 and was built to specifications drawn up by three of the crew. She lasted until 1933 and was regarded with a great deal of affection by the people of the town. The boathouse, built in 1903, is situated halfway between Llandudno's two shores. The most tragic and dramatic call received by the Llandudno boat was to the stricken *Thetis* when nothing could be done for the 100 men lost.

Before the late 1850s when the RNLI took over the Anglesey lifeboat services the Anglesey Lifesaving Association had saved over 400 lives. There has been a boat at Moelfre since 1830. The Cemlyn boat moved to this site and stayed here until 1867 when she was replaced by the *London Sunday School and Charles Scone*. The *Lady Vivian* took her place in 1874, and two boats followed, each called the *Star of Hope*. This picture is of the *Star of Hope* built in 1892. She was propelled by sail and oar and was a self-righting vessel. She left Moelfre in 1910. The Moelfre station has a distinguished history and is renowned worldwide for the bravery of its crew. Special mention must be made of Coxswain Dick Evans whose fascinating life and exploits are recorded in Ian Skidmore's book *Lifeboat VC* (David & Charles, 1979).

A very rare photograph of one of the early lifeboats at Bull Bay, Amlwch, Anglesey, *c.* 1867. It is either the *Eleanor* or the *Curling*. The station was built in 1867 and the cost was borne by a gift from a Miss Holt of Anglesey, while the site was donated by the Marquess of Anglesey. John Hughes was appointed coxswain. *Eleanor* went on her last mission in 1879. *Curling* served for five years and was replaced with another of the same name. A new boathouse with a slipway opened nearby in 1904. The last recorded service provided by the station was in 1924 and it closed on 22 April 1926.

Off Holyhead there are very busy shipping lanes of Liverpool-bound traffic and Irish packet craft. The area around Holyhead has seen numerous wrecks throughout the ages, particularly in the age of sail before sophisticated navigational aids. The first expressed need for a lifeboat came in 1825 from the Revd James Williams. This led to the formation of the Anglesey Lifesaving Association, which was later taken over by the RNLI. In 1875 a house with a slipway was constructed and the *Thomas Fielden* appeared. A second station was opened in 1890. One of the first steam lifeboats, the *Duke of Northumberland*, arrived in 1892, but after less than a year it moved to New Brighton. It returned in December 1897 and remained until 1922. From 1850 to 1969 the Holyhead station saved 1,108 lives and her crews have won 4 gold, 31 silver and 9 bronze medals.

Concentrated in an isolated spot at Llanddwyn on the coast of Anglesey there were three major aids to the safety of shipping: pilot houses, a lighthouse and the Llanddwyn lifeboat station. This was the first station to be established in Anglesey in 1826. In 1836 the boat was transferred to Caernarfon, but launching difficulties led to its return in 1840. The *John Gray Bell* was replaced by the *Richard Henry Gould*, the boat being launched in this photograph in 1906. She was launched with serious intent only ten times during her lifetime of twenty-two years. The station was closed in 1907.

In the early years of the nineteenth century Porthdinllaen harbour, on the south of Caernarfon Bay, rivalled Holyhead to become the main packet port to Ireland. The amount of busy sea-going traffic in this area meant that lifeboat assistance was needed on many occasions. In one day in 1844 ten vessels were driven ashore near Porthdinllaen, of which four were completely lost. A lifeboat station was opened in 1864. This is the launch of the *Charles Henry Ashley* after her naming ceremony, 12 August 1949.

The Barmouth station was opened in 1828 after local pressure. *Jones Gibb* arrived at the station in 1885 and was replaced in 1905 by the boat seen here, the *Jones Gibb II*. This new 38 ft boat was too big for the boathouse, which had to be enlarged; two men were killed in blasting operations. In 1939 the *Jones Gibb II* was replaced by the *Lawrence Arden Stockport*. During the Second World War the boat was called out twenty times to save the crews of ditched aircraft. In 1949 she was replaced by *The Chieftain*.

CHAPTER NINE

LIGHTHOUSES

The Point of Ayr lighthouse is on the shores of the River Dee marking the mouth of this treacherous estuary.
This once very busy estuary is now quiet, and the shipping lanes are busy no more.
The first lighthouse built in the area was constructed in 1777 at a cost of £353 18s 4d. The light has long
since ceased to function but it is historically interesting because it contains one of the earliest lanterns used
in Wales. It was not always a resounding success as a lighthouse and was replaced by a lightship in the
estuary in 1883. Trinity House took over from the Point of Ayr Lighthouse Trustees in 1819 and there was a
considerable amount of rebuilding in 1820. In 1891 a third and final house was built on the high-water
mark. This is the one seen there today, a five-storey 'desirable residence'.

Perched precariously on the precipitous cliffs of the Great Orme is the strong, square, castellated structure of the Great Orme lighthouse. The need for the light was first fully expressed on 3 December 1861 by K. Parker in a letter to Trinity House. The light first shone on 1 December 1862. The whole structure was designed by G. Lyster, chief engineer of the Mersey Docks and Harbour Board. The original equipment was still on site, carefully preserved, in 1979. The light last shone on 22 March 1985 when the lighthouse reverted to the ownership of the Mersey Docks and Harbour Board. It sold the property which is now a private hotel with spectacular sea views.

This lighthouse at Penmon Point, Anglesey, marks the north entrance to the Menai Strait and is situated in the narrow stretch of water between Penmon Point and Ynys Seiriol (Puffin Island). It was built between 1835 and 1838, largely in response to the great tragedy of the wrecking of the *Rothsay Castle* on 8 August 1831 when over 100 lives were lost. The base of the structure is stepped to reduce the effects of upsurging seas. A distinguishing feature is a castellated stone parapet as opposed to the usual railings in the gallery. The tower has not been manned for years, but the continuous light is controlled by the Holyhead centre, and there are proposals for it to become solar powered.

The harbour of Amlwch was blasted out of the rock to facilitate the export of copper from what was then Europe's biggest copper mine at nearby Parys Mountain. The two piers built at the harbour entrance each had an octagonal tower with small lanterns protruding from their roofs. A square tower was built at the end of an outer pier in 1817 which was longer than the other two (150 ft). The light on this tower was 28 ft above the high-water mark. The existing tower was built in 1853.

The lighthouse on the Holyhead Breakwater was built sometime between 1845 and 1873 and designed by John Hawkshaw. It is 63 ft high and, unusually, is a square structure. The light here is operated by Trinity House from the Holyhead centre.

One of the most photographed lighthouses in Great Britain, the South Stack is situated on the summit of an island off the north-west of Holyhead Island, a site of great scenic beauty and grandeur. It is connected to Holyhead Island by a rigid bridge. The first lighthouse was built at South Stack in 1809. The present lighthouse was designed by Joseph Nelson, and the constructing engineer was Daniel Alexander. It cost approximately £12,000 to build. In 1984 the lighthouse became automatic, operated from the Holyhead control centre.

Llanddwyn Island lighthouse marks the western entrance to the Menai Strait and was first built in 1846. The tower resembles the structure of the many Anglesey windmills and may indeed have been a windmill originally, or simply designed by a windmill designer. The light room was at the front of the tower. The community of Llanddwyn Island also served as lifeboat men and crews of pilot boats. The lantern from the base was discontinued in 1975 and a light was placed on top of the structure. The cottages are now used as craft workshops as a tourist attraction.

Point Lynas lighthouse, Anglesey. A lighthouse was first established here in 1779 at a site some 300 m to the south of the present position. The move obviated the need for a tower, because the present site is the highest point in the vicinity. It was designed and built by Jesse Hartley, engineer to the Mersey Docks and Harbour Board. It is now unmanned and the automatic light is controlled from Holyhead.

The Skerries lighthouse. On the north-west tip of Anglesey there is a small and dangerous outcrop of rocky islets, the Skerries. The original lighthouse was built here in 1716, but there had been a previous structure since 1685, paid for by a group of Liverpool merchants. The lighthouse has had a chequered financial history, with its owners locked in conflict with Trinity House, who wished to purchase it at a deflated price. In 1844 Trinity House finally purchased it for £444,984, an enormous sum of money in those days. The lighthouse was then restored by James Walker. The light shines at 119 ft above high water. It is no longer manned, but automatically controlled from Holyhead. The houses are used by the RSPB as summer dwellings for its officials.

The tower on the southern tip of Bardsey Island off the Lleyn Peninsula is almost 100 ft high and was built in 1821. Joseph Nelson was the engineer and builder. Again, unusually, it has a square structure. It cost £2,950 to build. The house is now unmanned and the former keepers' dwellings are leased to the Bardsey Island Trust. The light is automatic and controlled by the Holyhead control centre.

The St Tudwall's light marks the north end of Cardigan Bay at Abersoch. The tower, which is 35 ft high, was built in 1877. It is now a small unmanned light and the original keepers' cottages are privately owned as holiday homes.

CHAPTER TEN

TRAINING SHIPS

A familiar and beautiful sight in the Menai Strait during the Second World War and up until 1953 was the training ship Conway. We see her here in the Mersey along with two of her sister training ships. The Conway is nearest to the camera, in the middle distance is the Akbar, formerly the Cornwall, and in the far distance the Indefatigable. HMS Conway was regarded with a great deal of affection by the people of North Wales, not least because of the tragic way of her going. Before the Conway arrived in the Menai Strait, another training ship, the Clio, was moored off Bangor from 1877 to 1920.

During the latter half of the nineteenth century concern was felt for the plight of 'street arabs', vagrants and youths with little purpose. Committees were established to finance institutions and refurbish seaworthy sailing vessels to accommodate these children and provide a trained and efficient workforce for the Royal Navy and the Mercantile Marine. The Clio was one of those vessels. The Conway, on the other hand, was established 'to provide an academy for the maintenance and education of the children of destitute and deceased merchant officers and seamen', additionally 'receiving other boys on payment of an annual sum for the purpose of making the institution partially self-supporting'. The Conway was, therefore, primarily concerned with giving boys the necessary foundation for subsequent officer status.

Some twenty or so training ships were established in the major ports of Great Britain.

Two photographs of the *Clio* at her moorings off Bangor Pier, *c.* 1910. In 1877 the *Clio*, a spar-decked Corvette of some sixteen guns, was moored at this point between Bangor Pier and Glyn Garth. Originally she had been destined for moorings off Mostyn in the Dee estuary, but there was a change of mind and a more agreeable environment was chosen. The ship was built of African oak and painted black and white. The three-masted vessel cost £7,000, which had been raised by public subscription and private donation. An Industrial Training Ship for children found begging or receiving alms, or found wandering homeless or without a guardian, she was capable of catering for 250 boys who came principally from the large industrial conurbations. The ship acquired an unfair reputation as a floating 'borstal' and her reputation as such lived on long after she had gone. The author recalls being threatened with the 'training ship' on many occasions following misbehaviour during his childhood in the 1930s. It is true that local miscreants, e.g. truants and apple scrumpers, could be sentenced to short periods of detention on the *Clio*. During the early years of this century her condition slowly deteriorated to the extent that a large sum of money was required to repair her. She was withdrawn from service and was broken up alongside Garth Pier in April 1920.

The training ship *Indefatigable* in the Mersey, *c.* 1914. The original *Indefatigable* (top) was a fifty-gun frigate, launched in 1848. Her active service life was curtailed because of the introduction of steam frigates into the Royal Navy. In 1857 she was paid off and in 1860 plans to convert her to steam were abandoned. In 1865 she sailed to the Mersey to join the other training ships moored there: the *Conway, Akbar* and *Clarence*. She never became a certified industrial school, so no government grants provided for her upkeep. She was financed by a subscription list and by donations. Intended for poor boys of good character, she was thus different from the *Conway*, which provided officer training, and the *Clio*, which accommodated 'vagrants'.

In 1914 the wooden ship was broken up and replaced by the steel-built *Phaeton*, seen below. She existed until 1947 when she was broken up, but in 1941 the school (not the ship) was transferred to Plas Llanfair, Anglesey. The school was finally closed in 1996.

During her life as a training ship HMS *Conway* prepared thousands of boys for careers at sea. A training ship known as the *Conway* had served in the Mersey and Menai Strait since 1859. She had been in fact three different ships and the last one had originally been a ninety-gun battleship, the *Nile*, which had been in service since 1867. She was laid down in Devonport in 1827 and was launched in 1839. Even at her launch she was surplus to needs and obsolete. She saw active service when she was used to blockade the Russian Fleet in the Gulf of Finland. Below: she was moved from the Mersey to the Strait in 1941 to escape the blitz. Her first moorings were off Bangor and eventually in 1949 her last moorings were off Plas Newydd, the home of the Marquess of Anglesey, where she stayed until 1953.

On 14 April 1953 *Conway* was towed from her moorings by two tugs, *Dongarth* and *Minegarth*, and was destined for Cammell Lairds' Yard at Birkenhead where she was to be refitted. The passage through the Swellies was a difficult one and the suspension bridge and banks were lined with people watching the splendid old vessel's progress. Suddenly the *Conway* stopped moving; held by a fierce current she began to drift astern taking the tugs with her. The tow rope suddenly snapped and with a shuddering jolt the *Conway* ploughed into the bank on the Caernarfon shore. Her back was broken and she was beyond redemption.

In the shadow of Telford's suspension bridge is the wreck of HMS *Conway*, formerly HMS *Nile* which had been laid down at Devonport in October 1827. Hundreds of people had witnessed her demise and she is still remembered with a great deal of affection throughout North Wales. She was later set on fire to keep her from marauding souvenir seekers.

Seen here at Bristol before the turn of the century is the three-masted barque *Eivion*. She was built by Carbourne, Graham & Co. for the North Wales Shipping Co. of Caernarfon in May 1879. In 1887 she was sold to W. Thomas & Sons of Liverpool, and resold in 1894 to R. Thomas & Co. of Liverpool, Criccieth and Caernarfon. On her way to Tocapilla in 1904 carrying coal, the most feared of sea disasters occurred – she caught fire. Fortunately the ship *Lonsdale* was at hand and rescued the crew.

The *Wynnstay*, an iron three-master built in 1884 for D.W. Daniels of Liverpool by Russell & Co. at Port Glasgow. She changed hands in 1884 but returned to Welsh owners W. Thomas & Co. (Dominion Ship Co. Ltd) of Liverpool. She was wrecked on 30 July 1910 on Serrano Island at the entrance to Iquique while outward bound from Swansea. Two of her crew were drowned.

The *Cadwgan* was built in 1885 by William Doxford of Sunderland and was owned by Robert Thomas & Co. In 1910 she was sold on to a French sailing company and she ended her days 'hulked' in the Pacific. In this photograph she is bound for Iquique.

The *Carnedd Llewelyn* was built in 1891 by Russell & Co. of Greenock. Named after one of the mountains in the Snowdonia range, she was managed initially by Rogers & Co. of Liverpool but R. Hughes and Jones & Co. of Liverpool became her managers in 1892. She set sail from Caleta Buena for Falmouth on 19 February 1908. On 23 February she was seen by the *Quelpeu* but was never seen again.

The *Nellie Bywater* in Canning Dock, Liverpool, 1938. A wooden schooner, she was built in 1873 by an Amlwch builder, W. Thomas, at Milton in Cumbria. Her owner from 1922 was W. McKibbin of Whitehaven.

The *Emma and Esther* owned by Royle & Co. of Connah's Quay. She was built in 1871 and was broken up at Connah's Quay in 1930.

The *Cambrian Princess* was a three-masted iron ship of 2,437 tons and was built as the *Manydown* of Liverpool by Oswald Mordant, Southampton, in 1884 for E. Balis and Co. of Liverpool. She was sold to Welsh owners William Thomas & Co. of Liverpool in 1904 and renamed the *Cambrian Princess*. In 1913 she was sold to Norwegian owners and was dismasted in 1914 before being sold to French owners in 1915.

The *M.A. James* was built in 1900 by the famous David Williams of Porthmadog. She was owned by Captain W.I. Slade who sailed out of Appledore, Devon. During the Second World War she was used in the barrage balloon service, and she ended her days as a hulk at Appledore.

CHAPTER TWELVE

PLEASURE STEAMERS

At Llandudno Pier passengers wait to embark on one of the North Wales pleasure steamers, probably La
Marguerite, *c. 1910. From 1821 to 1963 these steamers provided cruises around the coast and into the Menai
Strait as far as Menai Bridge. They also brought thousands of day-trippers into the area from the Lancashire coastal
towns and the industrial north-west providing a much-needed boost to the developing holiday and tourist industry.
From the early years of the nineteenth century various companies have provided this service. The first one of
note was the St George Steam Packet Co., founded in 1821. The City of Dublin Steam Packet Co. took over
from them in 1843. In 1881 the Liverpool, Llandudno and Welsh Coast Steamboat Co. was formed and ten
years later it became the familiar Liverpool and North Wales Steamship Co.
In the early days, in the 1820s, conditions on the steamers were, to say the least, very primitive. The* Prince
Llewelyn *of the St George Steam Packet Co. was described by a contemporary as 'a shameful hulk, devoid of
shelter or accommodation other than that of a small cabin aft, and what screen there might be on the lee
side of a singularly tall funnel'. This is in sharp contrast to the luxuries afforded passengers when* La
Marguerite *and* St Tudno *joined the fleet as the century turned.*

A stormy night, an obdurate and drunken captain and an old, unseaworthy ship combined to make 13 August 1831 a tragically memorable one in the history of North Wales shipping. The *Rothsay Castle*, a wooden paddle steamer with a clipper bow, two masts and a single funnel, was no match for the combination of circumstances and sank with great loss of life on the Dutchman's Bank in the Menai Strait. Only twenty-three of the 130 passengers survived, and the graves of the lost are in Beaumaris churchyard. The loss of this boat led to new safety measures, including regulations and controls on the building and maintenance of this sort of vessel. The most obvious and lasting outcome was the Penmon lighthouse, seen here with a passing pleasure steamer and Puffin Island in the background.

In 1891 the first *St Tudno* was replaced by *St Tudno II*, which could accommodate over 1,000 passengers on her three decks. Built by the Fairfield Shipbuilding and Engineering Co. of Govan, she was launched on 9 April 1891. She was used as a troopship during the First World War, and was broken up in 1922 after a service life of thirty-one years.

The *St Elvies* was built by Fairfields at Govan and was delivered to the North Wales coast in 1896. She was 566 tons gross, with a speed of 18½ knots and had accommodation for just under 1,000 passengers. In 1915 she was requisitioned for minesweeping duties and returned to the company in March 1919. She worked for the company until 1930 when she was sold and broken up. In this photograph she is leaving Liverpool for her last trip before going to the breakers.

This handsome paddle steamer, *Snowdon*, was built by Laird Bros. of Birkenhead in 1892 for the Snowdon Passenger Steamship Co. Ltd of Liverpool. In 1899 the Liverpool and North Wales Steamship Co. Ltd took over the Snowdon company and acquired the *Snowdon*. She was one of the smaller vessels in the company with a certificate for 462 passengers and a speed of 14 knots. During the First World War she was a minesweeper working from Dover to Harwich, returning to North Wales in 1919. In 1931 she was broken up in Port Glasgow.

La Marguerite passing through the Strait at Penmon Point between Puffin Island and Anglesey, *c*. 1920. The Trwyn Du lighthouse is on the left. *La Marguerite* was built in 1894 by the Fairfield Co. Her early life was spent on the Thames where she was by far the largest and finest steamer the river had known to that date. She moved to North Wales in 1904. Licensed to carry 2,077 passengers the ship was the pride of the North Wales fleet. Her size and luxurious appointments made her a great favourite with the thousands of people who voyaged with her each season. She would leave Liverpool at 10.45 each morning and call at Llandudno, Beaumaris and Bangor, reaching her destination at Menai Bridge at 2.35 p.m. Below is a photograph of her captain, John Young, inset in a Menai Strait view. *La Marguerite* served as a troopship in the First World War, a sad duty. She was superseded in the Strait by *St Tudno III* in 1926 and was broken up at Briton Ferry.

St Elian at Rhyl Pier, *c.* 1910. Known originally as the *Southampton*, she was the property of the Southampton, Isle of Wight and South of England RMSP Co. She was built in 1872 and purchased by the L & NWSS Co. in July 1907 and renamed. Her top speed was 12 knots and she had a relatively small passenger capacity of 272. She was used mainly for short excursions. Although she looked a frail and flimsy craft, she lasted up to 1915. After forty-three years of service she was broken up at Briton Ferry.

The first *St Trillo* was bought in 1909 and was the last paddle boat to join the company. She had been built in 1876 as the *Carisbrooke* for a Southampton company and had served with the Colwyn Bay and Liverpool SS Co. for three years as the *Rhos Trevor*. She had a speed of 12 knots and could carry 463 passengers. During the First World War she was a minesweeper and returned to the Welsh coast in 1919. After a further two years' service she was sold to Spanish owners who renamed her *San Telmo*.

In 1922 the company bought a German-built minesweeper which had seen no war service because it had not been completed in time. Named *Hormun* she had been working for the Hamburg Amerika line in the Elbe. The company renamed her *St Elian II*. Her gross capacity was 528 tons and she was capable of carrying 528 passengers at a speed of 15 knots. Bought by an Italian company in 1927, she lived out the rest of her life in the Mediterranean, first as the *Partenhope* and then as the *Ischia*.

SAILINGS FROM LLANDUDNO PIER

(weather and other circumstances permitting, subject to alteration without notice)

Leaving	Daily (Suns. included)	Due Back	Return Fare (Including Pier Tolls)	Leaving a.m.	WEDNESDAYS	Due Back p.m.	Return Fare (Including Pier Tolls)
p.m. 1.15	T.S. "St. Tudno" or "St. Seiriol" **MENAI BRIDGE** (1 hour ashore)	p.m. 5. 0	7/6	10.15	T.S. "St. Seiriol" **DOUGLAS (I.O.M.)** (About 2¾ hours ashore)	8. 0	20/-
	SUNDAYS			a.m. 10.45	M.V. "St. Trillo" **Morning Cruise** ...	p.m. 12.15	4/-
a.m. 10.45	M.V. "St. Trillo" **Morning Cruise** ...	p.m. 12.15	4/-	p.m. 2.30	**MENAI BRIDGE** (About ½ hour ashore)	p.m. 6.00	7/6
p.m. 2.45	**Afternoon Cruise** ...	p.m. 4.45	6/-	p.m. 7.30	**Evening Cruise** ...	p.m. 9.00	4/6
p.m. 7.30	**Evening Cruise** ...	p.m. 9. 0	4/6				
	MONDAYS				**THURSDAYS**		
a.m. 10.45	M.V. "St. Trillo" **MENAI BRIDGE** (3½ hours ashore) Return 3.45 p.m. by "St. Tudno"	p.m. 5. 0	7/6	a.m. 9.30	T.S. "St. Seiriol" **LIVERPOOL** (2 hours ashore)	p.m. 4.30	10/-
p.m. 2.45	**Afternoon Cruise** ...	p.m. 4.45	6/-	a.m. 10.45	M.V. "St. Trillo" **MENAI BRIDGE** (3½ hours ashore) Return 3.45 p.m. by "St. Tudno"	p.m. 5. 0	7/6
p.m. 6.00	**MENAI BRIDGE** Circular Tour Out Boat, Return Crosville Bus.	p.m. 10.20 or 10.40	7/- Children 3/6	p.m. 2.45	**Afternoon Cruise** ...	p.m. 4.45	6/-
	TUESDAYS			p.m. 6.00	**MENAI BRIDGE** Circular Tour Out Boat, Return Crosville Bus.	p.m. 10.20 or 10.40	7/- Children 3/6
a.m. 10.15	T.S. "St. Seiriol" **DOUGLAS (I.O.M.)** (about 2¾ hours ashore)	p.m. 8. 0	20/-				
a.m. 10.45	M.V. "St. Trillo" **MENAI BRIDGE** (3½ hours ashore) Return 3.45 p.m. by "St. Tudno"	p.m. 5. 0	7/6	a.m. 10.45	**FRIDAYS** M.V. "St. Trillo" **Morning Cruise** ...	p.m. 12.15	4/-
p.m. 2.45	**Afternoon Cruise**	p.m. 4.45	6/-	p.m. 2.30	**MENAI BRIDGE** (About ½ hour ashore)	p.m. 6. 0	7/6
p.m. 6.00	**MENAI BRIDGE** Circular Tour Out Boat, Return Crosville Bus.	p.m. 10.20 or 10.40	7/- Children 3/6	p.m. 6.00	**MENAI BRIDGE** Circular Tour Out Boat, Return Crosville Bus.	p.m. 10.20 or 10.40	7/- Children 3/6

An advertising leaflet of 1960 showing sailing times from Llandudno Pier.

St Tudno III arrived in 1926 and was bigger than any other steamer previously employed on the route. The passenger accommodation was greater than *La Marguerite* by some 400 passengers. She was 329 ft long, beam 44 ft, gross tonnage 2,326. The photograph above shows her on her maiden trip, leaving Liverpool for North Wales.

St Tudno III docked at Menai Bridge, awaiting her passengers. Power was provided by two oil-fired boilers and her 19 knot speed coupled with her excellent on-board facilities made her a very popular ship, though she did not inspire the same sort of affection as *La Marguerite*. Her increased size and subsequent manoeuvrability problems meant she had to stop calling at Bangor and Beaumaris. On 25 March 1963 the *St Tudno III* was sold for demolition and she departed for Ghent on 13 April, never to be seen again. An era was coming to an end!

The second ship to be named the *St Seiriol* passing under Telford's Menai Suspension Bridge. *St Seiriol I*, a minesweeper, was built in 1914 and was mined and sunk off Harwick in 1918. *St Seiriol II* was built by Fairfields in 1931 to provide a support service for the *St Tudno*. In many respects she was a miniature version of the *St Tudno*. She played a significant role in the historic evacuation of Allied troops from the beaches of Dunkirk; in all she returned to the beach seven times and was only minimally damaged. In 1963 she was broken up.

On her maiden voyage the *St Trillo* enters Amlwch harbour, 1936. The intention was to name her *St Tysilio* but she appeared as *St Silio* and was renamed *St Trillo* after the war in 1945. She was small compared to the other ships in the fleet, but was still larger than many of her paddle steamer predecessors. She was 149 ft long, beam 27.1 ft and gross tonnage 314, capable of carrying 568 passengers. Her two funnels looked superfluous for a ship of her size and, indeed, her forward funnel was a dummy. She worked in the Bristol Channel for about five years and was then broken up in 1968, the last ship of the line to go. With her went a piece of history!

The *Greyhound* was built in 1895 at Messrs J. and G. Thomson's yard on the Clyde. She belonged to the Blackpool Passenger Steamboat Co. Ltd and ran from the Lancashire coast to Douglas and Llandudno. She also ran excursions from Preston to Llandudno and the Menai Strait. After the First World War, when she was a minesweeper, she returned to duty in 1919. In 1928 she moved to Belfast Laugh and in 1935 she was sold to a Turkish company and renamed *Buyuk Ada*.

The former Clyde steamer *Viceroy*, which was built in 1875. She was purchased by Mr Horton of the Colwyn Bay and Liverpool SS Co. Ltd and renamed the *Rhos Colwyn*. Her sister ships were the *Rhos Neigr* and the *Rhos Trevor*. She was the last survivor of this little fleet and was broken up in 1911. The *Rhos Neigr*'s remains can still be seen at low tide in Penrhyn Bay where she struck a rock, was beached and eventually broke up.

This elegant little ship, *Lady Orme*, broken up in 1939, had an intermittent career on the North Wales coast. She was originally called the *Fusilier* and spent one season in the Firth of Forth. She was not a large ship, with a length of 202 ft, beam 21 ft and gross capacity 251 tons. She appeared on the North Wales coast in 1935 and was based at Llandudno, owned by the Cambrian Shipping Co. Her Sunday trips were very popular, according to local legend, because she could sail out over the bar where the Welsh Sunday drinking laws did not apply. She also ran an excursion service between Llandudno and Menai Bridge. Her brief stay was from 1935 to 1936. In 1937 she returned, owned by the Orme Cruising Co. Again in 1938 she returned, as the *Crestawave*.

There have been passenger paddle steamers on the River Conway since the middle of the last century. The *St George* was probably the first to appear in about 1847. This small company ran a day trip service for tourists up the river. The quay at Deganwy was called the St George Quay, and even though she did not run from it, the company called itself the St George Co. In this busy scene on the shore at Deganwy after 1900 a screw steamer, the *Trefriw Belle*, is in the foreground with three of the St George fleet in the middle distance. In the background is Conway Morfa and Conway Mountain.

One of the St George paddle steamers on its way to the Trefriw Quay. It could be one of the four boats with a 'George' in its name: *St George* (1847), *Prince George* (1891), *New St George* (date unknown) and *King George* (1907). The fleet's funnels were yellow with a black top.

Two photographs of the quay at Trefriw, *c.* 1905. This was effectively the terminus for the day trip, though the boats went further upstream towards historic Llanrwst when tidal conditions allowed. Trefriw was a popular venue with the tourists. During the trip they enjoyed the views of the town of Conway with its two bridges and up the valley to Trefriw. Trefriw itself had a famous spa with medicinal waters, and there were lovely walks and picnic spots in the vicinity.

CHAPTER THIRTEEN

HOLYHEAD SHIPS

The first station in Holyhead was built in 1848 approximately a third of a mile from its present position. Packet boat passengers were carried to the Admiralty Pier by horse bus. The building of the harbour coincided with the building of the station and the Great Breakwater, which was completed in 1870. Rails were laid to the pier in 1851. The LNWR purchased the hotel, the Eagle and Child, and renamed it the Royal Hotel. In 1876 plans were approved for a massive rebuilding programme for a new railway station and a hotel. These were completed and officially opened on 17 June 1880 by HRH The Prince of Wales (later Edward VII) and a large ornate clock, built by James Joyce of Whitchurch, Shropshire, was erected in the passenger area to mark the occasion. The hotel was closed in 1951. Freight traffic ceased in 1968 and the hotel was demolished in 1978 to make way for station improvements.

In 1849 the Chester and Holyhead Railway Company secured the contract to carry mail to Holyhead from London, reducing the journey time to approximately 9 hours 35 minutes from the coach service of up to 27 hours.

The Royal Mail steamer *Leinster* on a postcard published by the City of Dublin Steam Packet Co. at the turn of the century. The *Leinster* was a twin-screwed steamer launched in 1896, and her sister ships were the *Ulster, Munster* and *Connaught*. This quartet replaced four paddle steamers with the same names. The mail service to Ireland between Holyhead and Kingstown had been contracted to the CDSP since 1850. Each of the ships in the line contained large sorting offices so that the company's business could be continued while in transit. It lost the mail contract to the LNWR in 1920, and, as a consequence, went out of business. On 10 October 1918 the *Leinster* was torpedoed in broad daylight and 500 people were drowned.

This composite postcard sent in 1912 shows some of the early vessels on the Holyhead–Ireland route:

Cambria, an iron paddle steamer built in 1848 by Laird's of Birkenhead. Her original length was 207 ft 5 in, beam 267 ft 3 in, gross tonnage 590. In 1861 she was enlarged to length 244 ft, beam 27 ft 1 in, gross tonnage 759. She was in the service until 1884.

Violet, built by Laird's, with a hull of Crewe steel, in 1880. Length 300 ft, beam 33 ft 1 in, gross tonnage 1,035. She received a new engine in 1889. She served for twenty-two years until 1902. Her sister ship was *Lily*.

Olga was a steel twin-screw ship, again built by Laird's, in 1887. Length 301 ft 5 in, beam 33 ft, gross tonnage 970, she was capable of 15 knots. She lasted until 1908.

Around the turn of the century four ships joined the LNWR express passenger service between Holyhead and Dublin. The company was in direct opposition to the City of Dublin Steam Packet service which still held the coveted mail franchise. This is one of several ships called *Cambria* over the years. This *Cambria* was built in 1897 and was a steel twin-screwed vessel, 329 ft long, beam 39 ft 1 in, gross tonnage 1,842. She was capable of speeds in excess of 20 knots and served for twenty-eight years, which seemed to be the average life of a boat on the service. She finished in 1925.

The *Anglia* was the second of the quartet and she joined the fleet in 1900. Length 329 ft, beam 39 ft 1 in, gross tonnage 1,862, she was sunk in November 1915 after hitting a mine in the English Channel.

This postcard image was used to depict three different ships, the only difference being the name appended to the picture.

The *Rostrevor* was built in 1895, the first of three ships of very similar size, appearance and specifications. Her builder was William Denny, Dumbarton. Length 272 ft 1 in, beam 35 ft 1 in, gross tonnage 1,094 and capable of 18 knots, the *Rostrevor* stayed with the service until 1926.

A steel twin-screw ship, the *Connemara* was built as sister to the *Rostrevor* by Denny in 1897. Gross tonnage was 1,105, length 272 ft 1 in, beam 35 ft 1 in and top speed 18 knots. She was lost in tragic circumstances on Friday 3 November 1916, when ninety-four people lost their lives. On passage from Greenore to Holyhead with ninety people on board and a cargo of cattle and horses she was struck amidships by the steamship *Retriever* bound from Garston to Newry with a cargo of coal. Both ships sank immediately with only one survivor, a member of the *Retriever*'s crew, James Boyle, who struggled ashore at Cranfield Point.

The *Galtee More* was a slightly larger version of the *Connemara*, her sister ship, again built at Dumbarton by Denny. Length 276 ft 1 in, beam 35 ft 1 in and capable of 18 knots, she lasted twenty-eight years and was disposed of in 1926.

In 1921 the company built four more ships of the same class and with the same size and appearance: *Anglia, Hibernia, Cambria* and *Scotia*. They were all twin screw-turbine craft with the same overall dimensions of 392 ft, tonnages varied around the 3,450 mark, beam 45 ft and they were capable of 25 knots. Building a complete class at the same time was a very costly venture for the company. The *Anglia* left the service in 1934, the *Hibernia* in 1948, the *Cambria* in 1949. Tragically the *Scotia* was sunk with great loss of life at Dunkirk on 1 June 1940 during the evacuation of BEF troops. Because of this the ship is remembered with a great deal of affection by the people of Anglesey, many of whom lost friends or relatives in the tragedy.

The third of the four was the *Hibernia*, seen here leaving Dublin (North Wall), *c.* 1910. She was built by William Denny, Dumbarton, in 1900. Length 329 ft, beam 39 ft 1 in, gross tonnage 1,862, and capable of 21/22 knots, during the First World War she was requisitioned for war service and became an armoured cruiser called HMS *Tara*. On 5 November 1915 she was torpedoed in the Mediterranean off the coast of Egypt. She sank in eight minutes and twelve lives were lost. The photograph below is a commemorative photograph of the ship's crew on their return to Holyhead. They had spent 135 days in the desert as prisoners of war guarded by hostile tribesmen who were commanded by Turkish officers.

Space precludes consideration of all the vessels on the Holyhead–Ireland routes, but mention must be made of a group of boats named after Irish mountains, the 'Slieve' boats. They were built after 1900, both by the LNWR and the LMS. There was the *Slieve More*, *Slieve Bawn*, *Slieve Bloom, Slieve Gallion*, all built between 1904 and 1908. The *Slieve Donard* (above) was built by Vickers of Barrow-in-Furness in 1922 for the LNWR. Smaller than the other ships in the fleet by some 100 ft, her length was 298 ft 9 in, beam 39 ft 1 in, gross tonnage 1,116 and top speed 15 knots. She left the service in 1954. Below is the *Slieve Bawn II*, built in 1937 for the London Midland and Scottish Railway.

CHAPTER FOURTEEN

CANALS

In 1791 a scheme was proposed for a canal system to link the Mersey and Severn rivers. Part of this system
would run through the industrial north-east of Wales, through the iron and coal producing areas of
Wrexham and Ruabon, and then continue on to Shrewsbury. The scheme did not achieve its objective in that
the Mersey and Severn were never joined, but a small self-contained system was created out of the proposal,
so that by 1806 there was a waterway between Chirk Bank and Pontcysyllte and from there a navigable
stretch went to Llangollen. The canal system went on to Chester and to the sea via Ellesmere Port.

The stretch between Chirk Bank and Pontcysyllte is famous because of the engineering feats performed
during its completion. The aquaduct at Chirk is impressive enough, but the spanning of the Dee Valley by the
Pontcysyllte aquaduct with Telford's iron trough is a monument to the Industrial Revolution – many think it
is a more impressive testimony than Ironbridge in Shropshire. Chirk and Pontcysyllte were described by
Samuel Smiles in his Lives of the Engineers as 'among the boldest efforts of human invention in modern
times' and later as 'the most impressive work of art he had ever seen'.

Chirk aquaduct was built in 1801 by Thomas Telford. This impressive engineering feat consisted of a cast-iron trough carrying the Shropshire Union Canal 65 ft over the Ceiriog Valley. The trough is set in a stone encasement. At the end of the aquaduct there is a mile-long tunnel built to preserve the view from Chirk Castle. Inside the tunnel there was a towpath so that the boatmen did not have to 'leg' through it. Alongside the aquaduct a viaduct was built 35 ft higher to carry the Chester–Shrewsbury railway line. This was opened to traffic in 1848.

Near the village of Froncysyllte the canal has to span the width of the valley. The alternative to impossibly deep 'cuts' and massive lock systems was an aquaduct. The Pontcysyllte aquaduct stands 120 ft above the valley bottom and is 1,000 ft long. Designed by Telford and opened in 1805, it is a cast-iron trough resting on a line of stone piers. It took ten years to build and is a monument to Telford's genius.

This is the Black Park dock inlet from the canal, *c.* 1905. At this wharf the quarry products, stone and slate, were loaded. The horse-drawn wagons of the Glyn Valley Tramway brought the minerals to this point. In the background there is a towpath bridge over the Black Park coal dock inlet.

The supremacy of the canal for commercial and industrial transportation was short lived in Wales. Canals had to compete with tramways and the expanding rail system. Canal transportation was relatively cheap and, we now recognize, certainly more environmentally friendly than other modes, but its weakness was the extremely leisurely pace at which goods were transported. As industries and commercial concerns expanded, the demand for a speedier transport system eclipsed the canals. After some years of neglect, the inland waterway became the province of the leisure industry.

CHAPTER FIFTEEN

AEROPLANES

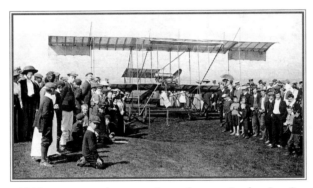

At 8 a.m. on 6 August 1910 a strange machine arrived over the sea at Penrhyn Bay. Out of the morning mist it soared over the golf course and landed close to the clubhouse. The first aeroplane to land in Wales! Out stepped a Boy's Own hero, W.G. Lorraine (aka Robert Jones), to be greeted by a very surprised club secretary wearing only his pyjamas and brandishing a toothbrush. Lorraine, an actor, had set out from Blackpool in his Farman biplane an hour and a half earlier aiming for Holyhead, but, because of sea mists, had missed his target by many a mile. His journey of some 63 miles had set a record for flights across the sea. News spread quickly and soon the aeroplane, a flimsy structure of plywood and canvas, was surrounded by an excited crowd, including several photographers. Special trams were put on by the local company and people crowded in from nearby Llandudno and Colwyn Bay. After a stay of several hours, during which the aeroplane was given an engineering inspection, Lorraine set off from the golf course, his ears ringing with the cheers of the excited crowd.

His next aim was to be the first aviator over the Irish Sea to Dublin and to this end he set off for Holyhead from where he would attempt the flight. Again he got lost in the mist over the sea and he is reputed to have fallen asleep as he attempted to navigate by following the coastline – a more sensible option would have been to follow the Chester–Holyhead railroad, a shorter and more direct route. He missed Holyhead and landed instead at Llanfair-yng-Nghornwy in the north of Anglesey with an empty petrol tank. The first aeroplane to land in Anglesey! On takeoff he crashed. The first aeroplane to crash in Anglesey! He was determined to complete the journey and, after a chapter of accidents, some of which would not have been out of place in a Keystone Cops' film, he set off from Holyhead for Dublin on Sunday 11 September. A few hundred yards from Howth Point near Dublin he ran out of fuel and had to ditch. He left his plane and swam to the shore. Within a matter of days the intrepid latter-day 'Biggles' was back on the West End stage.

In August 1911 the crowds gather again as an aeroplane lands on the beach at Rhos-on-Sea. This time the pilot is a Mr King. The photograph above is full of the atmosphere of the occasion with the Edwardian fashions of the day worn by the ladies leaning on the promenade railings. The obligatory parasols and wide-brimmed hats are protecting the wearers from the burning rays of the sun lest they become sunburned and look like the labouring classes. The scene contains so many modes of transport: an aeroplane, a motor car, a horse-drawn carriage, a perambulator and two bicycles. Over the years there have been several abortive attempts to build an aerodrome in the area of Rhos-on-Sea and Penrhyn Bay.

This undated photograph of Llandudno beach is described on the reverse simply as 'Blériot'. Blériot flew the English Channel in 1909. This could be him or more likely a plane called after him.

The arrival of an aeroplane in the early years of the century was the occasion for a great deal of interest and excitement. The crowds here on Llandudno beach are running to get a better view of the *Daily Mail* sea plane which has just arrived, July 1914. For the working man's average monthly wage it was possible to go for a trip in this plane.

An early photograph of what was to become a very important aeronautic connection for North Wales, taken during the First World War, *c.* 1915. It shows the interior of the service hangar at Queensferry Flying School on the flat land bordering the River Dee. This was later to become RAF Sealand, an important air base during the Second World War, and later still was the home of the US Air Force.

Great Britain's war effort during the Second World War was greatly enhanced by the work of a North
Wales factory at Broughton in Flintshire, the only aircraft factory in Wales. Vickers Armstrong built most
of its Wellington bombers at Broughton, over 5,000 in all, and in one year (1944–5) it built 235 Lancaster
bombers. Each month about 135 Wellingtons left the factory and, to break a record, it actually built a
Wellington from scratch in twenty-four hours. Approximately 3,000 of the 6,000 workforce were
women. When the war ended the factory turned to the manufacture of prefabricated housing and, in
three years, it made some 28,000. In 1948 De Havilland took over and aircraft construction was resumed
on the Mosquitos, Hornets, Doves and Vampire jets. Early Comets were also built in the factory, which is
now part of British Aerospace and latterly has been involved in making the wings for the European Air
Bus.

ACKNOWLEDGEMENTS

I should like to thank the following people for their help in the preparation of this book: Jim Boulton, Captain Gregory Caldecott, Phil Carradice, John Cowell, Mike Day, Geoff Ellis, David Evans, Mike Hitches, David Hughes, Brian Hurst, Lens of Sutton, Andrew Morley, Dr Ken Sherwood, Lionel Smith, Peter Wilding, the staff of Clwyd archives, Gwynedd archives and Llandudno library, and the authors of the many books consulted.

A quiet day in Mostyn Street, before 1910. Two trams of the original fleet are on a passing loop near St John's Church. The area with trees to the left of the church was eventually to become the site of the Marks & Spencer store. The sign on the wall proclaims 'Llandudno, the Queen of the Welsh Watering Places', a proclamation that has become the town's unofficial motto through the years.

BRITAIN IN OLD PHOTOGRAPHS

SUTTON'S PHOTOGRAPHIC HISTORY OF TRANSPORT

To order any of these titles please telephone our distributor, Littlehampton Book Services on 01903 721596
For a catalogue of these and our other titles please ring Emma Leitch on 01453 731114